Preventing Piracy

A Business Guide
to Software Protection

Preventing Piracy

A Business Guide to Software Protection

Ernest E. Keet

▲▼▲

ADDISON-WESLEY PUBLISHING COMPANY
Reading, Massachusetts • Menlo Park, California •
Don Mills, Ontario • Wokingham, England • Amsterdam •
Sydney • Singapore • Tokyo • Mexico City • Bogotá •
Santiago • San Juan

M. C. Varley, Sponsoring Editor

Hugh Crawford, Manufacturing Supervisor
Laura Skinger, Packaging Supervisor
Suzanne Stone, Design Coordinator
TKM Productions, Package Service

The author would like to thank Peter R. Lessler, Dunn & Bradstreet Corporation and Esther Schachter, Schachter and Froling for reviewing the manuscript and ADAPSO's 1981–3 Software Protection Committee for providing motivation and material for the book.

Library of Congress Cataloging in Publication Data

Keet, Ernest E.
  Preventing piracy.

  Bibliography: p.
  Includes index.
  1. Copyright—Computer programs—United States.
2. Computer programs—Patents. 3. Computer contracts—
United States. I. Title.
KF3024.C6K44   1984   346.7304'82   84-16776
ISBN 0-201-15047-6   347.306482

Contents

v

8
CUSTOMER CONTRACTS

9
NAMING YOUR SOFTWARE

10
PHYSICAL BARRIERS TO THEFT

11
PUBLIC POLICY AND THE FUTURE OF SOFTWARE PROTECTION

Preventing Piracy

A Business Guide to Software Protection

1

INTRODUCTION

Who This Book Is for and How to Read It

I am not a lawyer, I am a businessman. As a businessman, however, I have spent a considerable part of my life in areas where law, science, and industry meet. For twenty-two years I have been involved in creating and marketing a fascinating new form of intellectual property: computer programs and their related documentation, i.e., "software."

I have written this book for my colleagues in the software business. As a student of software protection, I know that their needs are not being met by the many legal texts on the subject. During the years I chaired a committee on software protection for the Association of Data Processing Service Organizations (ADAPSO), I was deluged with requests for specific advice. "Don't bother with the theory; what should I do now?" was the most common question.

The legal audience needs a different presentation than does the business audience. A good lawyer will revel in the ambiguities of the law and in the contradictions to be found in various court rulings. The business audience, in contrast, has little interest and even less time to pursue "on the one hand this, but on the other hand that" analyses. It is my opinion that the business community needs answers in addition to questions, even if the answers that are right today may be less so after new legislation, technologies, and court decisions unfold. Accordingly, where I take a risky position I will say so, but I will offer a position nonetheless. As this will put me at risk, please note that while I have done my best to provide authoritative and accurate information, this book is not intended to be nor should it serve as a substitute for legal advice or other expert services.

Knowing how precious the time of the business audience is, I have organized the book into separate but interrelated essays on software protection, each of which can be read individually. Chapter 3 provides a "cook book" approach to the subject, summarizing the recommendations given throughout the book. The other chapters explain the reasoning behind each recommendation. The Glossary at the back of the book is intended to define terms that are in the special province of the lawyer, the businessman, or the technician, but that are critical to the subject for all three. Because it will not interest everyone, issues of public policy (e.g., how patent or copyright disclosure can conflict with issues of national security) have been organized, wherever possible, into a separate final chapter.

I have tried to keep gender out of my writing but, as in the preceding paragraph, I have elected to use the term *businessman* rather than using alternative constructions, which are generally awkward. The word *man* is an ancient word meaning "human being." I will use *businessman* in this sense, for all my colleagues, male or female.

A Problem in the Making for Over Twenty Years

Twenty-two years ago, when I left graduate school for my first job (at IBM) there was no measurable market for packaged software, and custom development of software by professional service firms was in its infancy. Microcomputers did not exist as we know them, although the $500,000 general purpose business computers (e.g., IBM's 1401) then being sold had less memory, computing capacity, on-line disk storage, and software than does an IBM PC/XT, a modern desk-top device selling today for under $5000. Programs written for these early computers were unique and nontransferable because they were intimately tied to a specific machine type and device configuration. Operating systems (programs that control the computer, simplifying the programs that do the actual work) were primitive, requiring each program to repeat tedious instructions that controlled printers and other peripheral devices. High-level programming languages (e.g., FORTRAN and COBOL) had arrived on the scene in vendor-unique implementations, which lacked portability between machine types and hindered performance.

It is of little wonder that the problems associated with the protection of software loom larger today. In less than fifteen years, since IBM "unbundled" its software and hence created the independent software industry, software sales have jumped from a few million dollars per year to tens of billions. Operating systems and high-level language translators ("compilers") have coincidentally matured, making portable software more of a reality. Cheap microcomputers have opened up retail markets for published software unthinkable just five years ago. Large regional and nationwide professional service firms are creating software for others at an incredible rate, nearly $10 billion worth each year for the U.S. government alone. Corporate expenditures for data processing average about 2 percent of every sales dollar, or approximately a third of net profits. The percentage of these funds allocated to software purchase and development is now the single largest line item in the data processing budget, exceeding even the cost of the hardware.

But Is It a New Problem?

All of this economic activity has outstripped our ability to rationalize the process, to think through the financial and societal needs that these new businesses create. Is the production of software truly a new event, unparalleled in human existence? Are there analogies or tried paths we may be ignoring in fitting software into commercial and legal categories?

For example, is software tangible or intangible? If I create some software for you, who owns it—me or you? If you own it, can I again use the designs and processes that I used in creating it? If I own it, what did you pay for? If the designs and processes I used are my secret way of doing things, and hence the way I make a living, do they remain secret when I license them to you to use? What if I license the designs and processes to 10,000 people? How can 10,000 people know a secret and it still be a secret? Can you copyright a program? If so, does the copyright extend to both the "source code" used by the programmer and the "object code" created from the source code by a compiler? If I register a program for copyright do I give up my trade secret rights? Are mechanical forms of protection viable? What can I legally do to a software "pirate" (i.e., someone who uses my software without authorization)?

Suprisingly, in the years I spent with the Software Protection Committee of ADAPSO, I met very few businessmen or even lawyers who had answers to these questions. As a result, the business practices employed by some of our largest data processing firms are chaotic at best and wrong at worst.

Is It Worth Worrying About?

Is all this worth worrying about? I think so. Recently I was responsible for an acquisition that cost close to $70 million. The only asset of significance on the acquired company's (written-up) balance sheet was its software. If this asset were lost or its value written down as a result of an imperfect title, the result would be disastrous for seller and acquirer alike. While this seems obvious, I know of numerous cases where it would be difficult to counsel a company that its software has been kept out of the "public domain" or that employees and outside agents could not make legitimate claims on precious corporate "trade secrets."

Accordingly, my goal will be to both pose and answer the questions that you, in running your business, should be asking yourself, your staff, and your attorney. After a brief introduction and some important definitions, I will lay out a specific program in Chapter 3 that you can follow, even without a thorough understanding of the issues. The background data and the rationale for specific suggestions will be left to later chapters which, if you are fortunate enough to have both the power of delegation and a competent staff, you may choose to make assigned reading. Be forewarned, however, that there are judgment calls here that I believe should involve the highest levels of management. In short, I will advise and counsel, but the ultimate risk and judgment must be yours. I hope to be of service in the process.

2 PHILOSOPHY, DEFINITIONS, AND OVERVIEW

A Statement of Philosophy

Casual copying is not the problem

Popular concerns about software piracy border on paranoia. Just as cheap copying machines threw panic into the publishing industry, but caused little or no damage (book sales have risen steadily despite the proliferation of copiers), I believe the issue of unauthorized copying of programs by individuals will prove to be a tempest in a teapot. With a few important exceptions (e.g., video games), the legitimate user will not for long rely on software without formal documentation, updates, education, or maintenance.

It will be considered heresy by some, but I believe many software packages for personal computers owe some of their success to "piracy," i.e., many legitimate customers for such software decided to become so after an unauthorized trial. Do not misunderstand; *piracy* is merely a fancy word for theft. Nonetheless, the software vendor's primary goal is to make money, not to develop clever schemes to prevent copying. Increasing product distribution by legitimate means may meet this goal better than by using extraordinary means to restrict distribution. Many vendors have capitalized on the "try it, you'll like it" approach by offering limited capability demonstration versions of their products for a nominal fee.

Employee defections and unfair competition are more serious problems

Customers and prospects are generally not the enemy, and treating them as such is a dangerous and counterproductive practice. Most software misappropriation cases involve ex-employees or agents who become competitors. I suspect, however, that far more time is spent in the typical software company anticipating external problems than is spent planning for a feud within the "family." This is not to say that employees and agents should be distrusted, but merely that excess zeal in anticipating the unusual threat from a customer or prospect can result in damaging marketing practices. Conversely, sloppiness at home can be even more costly.

You can lose much more than just an employee

Prevention is the goal

A software company's assets are largely intangible. In addition to its software, these assets include the competence and knowledge of its employees, its customer base, and the value of its distribution channels. It is possible for a software company to have all four assets threatened at once when, for example, a group of employees sets up a competitive enterprise to sell a similar set of products or services to the same customer base through the same distribution channels. If this happens to you, you will probably cry "unfair competition" and/or "theft." If you have done your homework in advance so that you can prove either or both claims, you may be able to limit your loss to the departing employees. Even better, if your business practices discourage a raid on the corporation's intangible assets, you may avoid the problem altogether. That should clearly be your goal.

The laws are adequate

An economic incentive plus reasonable constraints

The underlying philosophy of this book is that the intangible assets of a business are threatened more by inadequate business practices than by inadequacies in the law. The legal protections that exist today may be convoluted and hard to understand, but they are adequate if they are properly applied. Similarly, encryption and physical protections have their place, but no protection scheme will defeat a determined thief who has sufficient economic incentive. The ultimate protection against theft by your customers lies in providing an economic bias toward honesty. For example, giving enough in the way of ancillary services, documentation, product updates, and education will cause the casual pilferer to join the ranks of legitimate customers. For employees and agents, the right approach is a fair and reasonable agreement on respective rights and obligations, coupled with a formal enforcement program.

In summary, a software vendor's goal should be to seek that point where the incentives to act honestly outweigh those to steal. This can be accomplished with a combination of legal protections, physical barriers, and economic incentives, all of which are available today. The ultimate solution to the software protection problem is to have all three in your arsenal. As Machiavelli said, "There is no comparison whatever between an armed and a disarmed man."

What Is "Software"?

Definitions are critical

No discussion of software or its protection can proceed without a clear understanding of what is meant by a "program," "software," "hardware," and so on. As we proceed you will discover that these definitional issues are critical, so bear with me for a brief, but important, digression.

Programs are processes...

A program is a set of instructions that directs the actions of a computer and its peripheral devices (printers, tape drives, disk drives, etc.). Programs are thus processes performed by the computer equipment (or "hardware") to achieve specific results. Programs may be created as the result of an intellectual undertaking (e.g., when a programmer writes a series of statements or symbols and creates "source code") or as the product of other programs that translate ("assemble" or "compile") source code into a form acceptable to the hardware, known as "object code." The resulting program may be contained in the circuitry of the hardware, "burned into" special memory cells of the computer (i.e., as "firmware"), or read into the computer's general memory as needed.

that can reside anywhere

Software is

In 1978, the World Intellectual Property Organization (WIPO), published a definition worth quoting here:

...a program plus

A "computer program" means a set of instructions capable, when incorporated in a machine-readable medium, of causing a machine having information processing capabilities to indicate, perform or achieve a particular function, task or result.

documentation

A "program description" means a complete procedural representation in verbal, schematic, or other form, in sufficient detail to determine a set of instructions constituting a corresponding computer program.

plus...supporting materials

"Supporting material" means any material, other than a computer program or a program description, created for aiding the understanding or application of a computer program, for example, problem descriptions and use instructions.

"Computer software" means any or several of the literary works referred to in the definitions of "computer program," "program description" and "supporting material."[1]

The critical points in all this verbiage are:

The medium is not the message

A program is a program regardless of where it resides; it does not change form when it is burned into a chip to control a home appliance or when it is delivered in "ROM" (read-only memory) to run a video game machine. Either way, it is still a program.

Software is everything not hardware

Software is an inclusive term, meaning the program, its description, and all supporting materials.

Software is a "literary work." In some cases, the output of the software is also an "audio-visual work." Why this is important will follow.

Tangible or Intangible?

You can sell tangibles, but you can only sell *rights* to intangibles

Is a program tangible or intangible? This is not a peripheral issue to the question of software protection. What you say you are selling has substantial impact on the degree to which you can protect any residual interest you have in the property. The answer also has a critical impact on the software enterprise, from taxation to import treatment to accounting.

If you can touch it, it's tangible

Legally, tangible personal property is defined as:

. . . that which may be felt or touched: Property capable of being possessed or realized; readily apprehensible by the mind; real; substantial; evident, such property as may be seen, weighed, measured, and estimated by the physical senses; that which is visible and corporeal; having substance and body as contrasted with incorporeal property rights such as franchises, choses in action, copyrights, and the like. It is visible, accessible, and easy to identify. "Tangible property" is synonomous with "goods, wares, and merchandise."[2]

The Supreme Court of Illinois held that an item is intangible if it cannot be ". . . stored, weighed, transported, handled, liquified, solidified, photographed, touched, or otherwise perceived by the senses in its own right or capacity separate and apart from mass or matter."

Tangible + intangible = tangible

It is clear that many items held to be "tangible" under the law derive much of their value from "intangibles." Whereas a book is clearly tangible, the copyrighted material in the book is, by definition, intangible. Thus, intangible property can be incorporated in tangible property and the result will be tangible in the eyes of the law.

**Programs, by them-
selves, are intangible**

Like the copyrighted material in the book, it is clear that a computer program by itself, apart from its physical representation, is intangible. It is a process that by itself cannot be "felt or touched." If the program is embedded in a tangible item, such as a silicon chip or a magnetic tape, for example, the combination is tangible.

**Software is
not unique**

Despite frequent special-interest protests to the contrary, software is not unique. Music is intangible, for example, but no one argues that a record with music recorded in the plastic is intangible. Software is similar in that it can exist either in its pure intangible form, as when it is transmitted over radio waves, or it can be a component of a physical offering. For example, software is recorded on a "floppy disk" that carries the software to the eventual computer in much the same way that a record carries the music to the record player.

**Self-serving claims of
uniqueness do more
harm than good**

The question of tangibility/intangibility is a red herring. The creation of software is a very conventional enterprise, non-unique in every respect. Those who seek to avoid taxation by claiming that software is unique do themselves and their industry a disservice. Legislatures and courts would do well to ignore these self-serving claims when deciding issues of software protection (and taxation).

**The form of the
transaction is key**

Relevant to ownership, protection, and taxation issues, however, is the fact that software, like music, scripts, graphical images, etc., can change hands in a variety of ways. Some industry practitioners (and several courts) have ignored the form of the transaction, looking rather for some basic rule that applies to all software transactions. However, the form of the transaction is indeed critical. Just as it is important to know whether a broadcaster has merely purchased the right to show a film or has acquired title to the film before you can answer questions on accounting, taxation, and property rights, so it is with software.

**An intangible process
transferred in a
tangible medium**

Software is a work of authorship that defines a machine process and, as such, it is intangible in its raw form but usually transferred in a tangible medium. As with all works of authorship, software enjoys copyright protection. As a process, software enjoys patent protection to the extent that other patent tests are met. If it is maintained in secrecy and commercially valuable, software enjoys state-by-state trade secret protections. Questions of property rights are largely contractual. As the valuable underlying property in such transactions is intangible, we must look to the form of the transaction to determine what rights in the property were actually transferred.

What Is Software Worth and Who Cares?

Up to $50 an instruction

Computer programs, fully documented and tested, cost between $5 and $50 per instruction to create. Application programs (inventory control, accounting, etc.) written in high-level languages average $6 to $12 per line of code, whereas "system software" (operating systems, compilers, database management systems), due to the intricacy of the programming and the need for compact and efficient routines, can cost up to five times as much. Annual maintenance costs for previously developed software are typically 20 percent of the initial investment.

In-house programs represent a substantial asset

Software developed for commercial markets (i.e., for sale to multiple users) requires a far greater degree of generality than does software developed for a specific user, and frequently involves two to five times as many instructions. As an example, a general ledger application written in COBOL for a specific company might involve 10,000 COBOL "source" statements for the main-line routines and another 30,000 statements for ancillary report-generation and inquiry routines. Most of the general-purpose packages on the market, however, contain hundreds of thousands of instructions. The generality built into the commercial offering allows the vendor to recoup his or her investment from hundreds or thousands of customers. This same generality saves the buyers huge amounts of pain and expense as their applications and technology evolve.

Commerical software can be worth $millions

Using these gross estimates, it is easy to see that an in-house application system can easily cost several hundred thousand dollars to develop, while a product developed for commercial distribution can run to millions. The total asset value of a medium-sized company's in-house software (which you will typically *not* see on any of its financial statements) can be substantial. If the primary business of the company is developing programs for sale, these hidden assets may represent the bulk of the company's true worth. Simply look at the prices being paid for software companies by private acquirers and by the public to see these off-balance-sheet values being monetized.

Most software never appears on a balance sheet

Software developed in-house is typically expensed, not capitalized. Even though the Financial Accounting Standards Board (FASB) has said that software "construction" (versus "research and development," a tenuous distinction) may (and soon must) be capitalized and depreciated,[3] few companies have thus far chosen to risk their banker's or the public's approbation by taking this more "aggressive" route. In many ways this is unfortunate, as small companies create assets they dare not represent on their balance sheets, which then penalizes current earnings on a dollar-for-dollar basis whenever they invest for the future. Smart investors have recognized this and hence extraordinary price/earnings multiples are awarded to publicly traded software companies.

Acquisitions and mergers uncover these assets

There is a quirk in accounting and tax regulations, however, that gives us a peek at the immense magnitude of these hidden assets. When assets are purchased from an independent party they may be "written up" for accounting purposes, i.e., their arms-length value can be recorded even if the assets did not appear on the balance sheet of the selling corporation. If these assets were not written up, and if the price paid exceeded the selling organization's book value, the difference would be recorded as "good will." Under IRS regulations, "good will" may be amortized over up to forty years but it is not a deductible business expense. As a result, there is tremendous incentive for a corporation that acquires hidden software assets to revalue them for book purposes and depreciate them (a deductible expense) on an accelerated basis. This is being done in nearly all software acquisitions. The result is a conversion of assets carried at zero value to assets carried at up to the price of the acquisition, not infrequently tens of millions of dollars.

The risks now are more than entrepreneurial

Suddenly, it is not only the small independent software developers whose assets are at risk. (In fact, as long as their profitability is not threatened by a question of title to these assets, they are little harmed; assets don't show on their financial statements!) The acquiring organizations have a huge interest in protecting both the on-going businesses they acquired and the accounting treatment they used. Anything other than a nuisance suit that made claim on the assets (software) acquired or, more typically, the use of these assets in the marketplace by third parties who claimed legitimate title could cause chaos.

What about the buyer of software? Is the buyer interested in the protection of purchased software? Absolutely.

The buyer usually accepts huge liabilities

First, the buyer of software may, under contract, accept tremendous liabilities. Most large-scale software packages are sold under contracts that obligate the buyer not to disclose or otherwise compromise the vendor's rights in the underlying product. Any breach of these contractual obligations could generate vendor claims for substantial business damages from the customer.

Embarrassed, fined, or jailed?

Second, statutory protections (e.g., copyright) generally apply to software purchases, whether or not a contract is involved. Once again, corporate laxness in preventing unauthorized copying of software (or worse, explicit or tacit sanctioning of copying) could lead to severe public embarrassment, substantial fines, and even prison sentences.

**Vendor viability
benefits the buyer**

A third, more subtle, issue also affects the software buyer—the viability of the vendor and of the software industry. A large measure of the value of a software product relates to its continual update and enhancement. If a vendor's product is misappropriated, the vendor loses at least one sale (and possibly thousands), suffering clear economic damage. This economic loss can lead to reduced product reinvestment, lessened support services, and even financial collapse.

**Yes, but tell it to the
software clubs**

Weakening or destruction of the vendor in turn harms the buyer, as he or she must then either pay more for the vendor's products and services or do without them altogether. A less viable business climate will drive away new capital and prevent the development of cheaper and better products. This simple economic tie between the well-being of the seller and the well-being of the buyer seems to be understood in the abstract, but completely ignored by otherwise honest individuals who see no harm, for example, in sharing microcomputer programs. Unfortunately, the exchange of proprietary software packages for microcomputers is widespread, and some "clubs" exist for this purpose alone.

In summary, there is a clear benefit to the vendor of computer software, the buyer, and to the general public in effectively protecting these intangible assets. The central question now becomes "How?"

Legal Protections: A Summary

Chapters 4, 5, and 6 describe the legal protections available to software. The following is a brief summary.

Three approaches

Patents, copyrights, and trade secrecy protections all can apply to software. Table 2.1 summarizes the characteristics of each.

**1. Forget about
patents**

Unless you have invented something truly new, unique, and nonobvious, patents do not apply. If you have invented such a work, your patent on pure software (without hardware) would need to survive a landmark decision by the Supreme Court before you would know for sure that it was valid. Even then, a U.S. software patent would be unenforceable in most jurisdictions outside of the United States. Finally, patent applications require disclosure, so filing would forever waive any trade secret claims you might have.

In contrast, copyright protections *are* applicable to software, are easy to get and protect, can be combined with trade secret and contractual protections, and *do* apply outside the United States. Copyrights are just that: a right to control the production of copies. Copyrights protect against duplication of a work of authorship but do not

Consideration	Copyright	Patent	Trade Secrecy	Contact Law
Duration	50, 75, or 100 years	17 years	Until disclosed	As agreed
Enforceable	Worldwide*	Nationwide	State-by-state	Worldwide*
Acquired by	Act of creation	Application	Agreement	Agreement
Lost by	Improper notice	Legal chal-lenge	Disclosure	Expiry or breach
Cost to obtain	Trivial	Significant	Trivial	Low
Cost to maintain	Trivial	Trivial	Significant	Low
Cost to defend	Moderate	Moderate	Significant	Moderate
Protects/prevents:				
Ideas & designs	No	Yes	Yes	Yes
Copying	Yes	Yes	No	Yes
Use	No	Yes	No	Yes
Independent invention	No	Yes	No	No
Distribution	Yes	Yes	Yes	Yes
Material must be:				
Unique	No	Yes	No	No
Novel	No	Yes	No	No
Used in business	No	No	Yes	No
Not generally known	No	Yes	Yes	No
Remedies available:				
Injunction	Yes	Yes	Yes	Yes
Statutory damages	Yes	No	No	No
Attorney's fees	Yes	Yes	No	No
Suitable for:				
Retail sales	Yes	Yes	No	No
Licensed use	Yes	Yes	Yes	Yes
Subject matter covered	Works of authorship	1. Machines 2. Articles of manufacture 3. Processes 4. Compositions of matter	Valuable business information	Anything

*with exceptions

TABLE 2.1   Alternative Legal Protections: A Summary

provide any protection for the underlying ideas or designs. The popular conception is that you do not violate a copyright if you change a line here or there and declare the new work as your own; this is not true. Even distant cousins of the original work enjoy copyright protection as either a copy or as a derivative work.

2. Copyright works, is easy, and may be all you need

Copyrights are now granted automatically under U.S. law, from the moment of creation. The copyright on the original work (e.g., the source program or an even higher-level description of the program) extends to its copies and derivatives (e.g., object programs). All you have to do is provide proper notice that the work is copyrighted. If the software also contains trade secrets and is distributed in confidence, the notice must say so as well.

Notice is important

Registration is a good idea

The software copyright can and should be registered, even though this is not specifically required, as registration brings additional remedies in the case of infringement. Registration requires a deposit of the software which, with careful planning, need not include the disclosure of any confidential information.

3. Trade secrecy laws are locally implemented

Trade secrecy and unfair competition laws exist on a state-by-state basis. Outside the United States, most of the industrialized world respects these same concepts, but the laws vary dramatically. As the vast majority of unfair competition cases involve ex-employees, trade secrecy should be viewed as a local protection against unauthorized misappropriation rather than as a worldwide system of legal protection.

Copright and trade secrecy can coexist

Trade secrecy laws protect against unauthorized disclosure; copyright laws protect against unauthorized copying. The two can coexist. While the current federal copyright law preempts all of the "equivalent rights" provided under state laws, this does not extend to those rights *not* provided by copyright, i.e., to the protection of the underlying designs, ideas, or processes. Some have argued that copyright implies disclosure and disclosure voids trade secrecy. While it is true that disclosure voids trade secrecy, the disclosure must be real, not implied. Merely availing yourself of the federally granted right to control the copying of your work will not conflict with your claim of secrecy; what counts is if you really keep it a secret.

It's not easy to maintain a trade secret

Software that is developed, maintained, and licensed under confidentiality agreements can and should enjoy trade secrecy protection. Even if your user-base grows to thousands, trade secrecy can apply. Your obligations to maintain the secrecy are formidable, however. Secrecy agreements are required with any employees, suppliers, agents, and customers who come in contact with the confidential material. Physical security, logs, and extensive labeling are essential. All this is worth it *if* you have designs, techniques, or ideas embedded in your software that provide a competitive advantage. If all you are concerned with is unauthorized copying, however, copyright and (where possible) customer contracts are sufficient.

Sales and Licenses: An Introduction

Transactions with customers are covered in detail in Chapter 8. The following is a very brief introduction.

Sales of goods are regulated

Post-sale restrictions on retail transactions are all but impossible

Retail sales of software are similar to retail sales of records, cassette recordings, and other products that have intangible material recorded in a tangible media. These transactions are subject to laws regulating consumer purchases, which generally prohibit unilateral waivers of warranties or liabilities. In addition, it is virtually impossible to place post-sale restrictions on the new owner of a product, other than those mandated by law. The so-called "license agreements" some vendors embed in their retail software packages are nothing of the kind, and it is wishful thinking to believe they do anything more than remind the user of applicable laws.

Licensing and selling are different

True licensing agreements between the customer and the vendor occur when the transfer involves only an exchange of intangible rights. In the case of software, the right involved is a right to use a proprietary process, and the tangible medium on which that process is embedded becomes incidental to the transaction. As the transaction involves neither a "sale" nor "goods," laws regulating the sale of goods do not apply. In these cases a contract defines the entire transfer, including the obligations of the customer to protect the material, secrets, copyrights, and so on.

Reverse engineering is perfectly legal

Obviously, whenever possible, software vendors would prefer to license the use of their software rather than sell copies. The license agreement can include prohibitions on disclosure, competition, and restrictions on use which would be otherwise permissible. When copies of a software product are sold without a contract the vendor must rely on copyright law and physical means of protection. In this circumstance there are no legal means to protect against "reverse engineering" or the discovery, by any legal means, of hidden designs or implementation techniques.

Retail sales and trade secrets can coexist

Even if there are no legal means to prevent the discovery of trade secrets in the delivered product, trade secrecy can exist. The mere ability of a secret to be disclosed does not eliminate its secrecy; only disclosure does. While this fact is of little benefit if a determined competitor unlocks the algorithms and techniques in your software, it *is* of great benefit in circumstances where relationships of trust exist, for example with employees and agents. As these relationships are the most common source of software misappropriation disputes, even the mass merchandiser of software can and should pay special attention to trade secrecy.

Dealing with Employees

Chapter 7 covers the subject of employee relations in detail. In general, however, most trade secret, unfair competition, and copyright infringement cases between employers and their ex-employees arise out of a lack of understanding of respective rights and obligations.

Implicit agreement may be no agreement

Yes, there are cases of outright theft, but these are rare. More commonly, the employer has failed to reach prior agreement with the employee on the exclusivity of ownership in ideas, designs, trade secrets, and confidential information. In many cases, the employer has also failed to recognize public policy shifts toward more freedom in the marketplace, which have brought limitations on post-employment constraints.

Employee rights are changing

The burden today is on the employer rather than on the employee. Blanket noncompete agreements, for example, have been outlawed in some states and are difficult to enforce in all others. Court cases have extended the rights of employees to information, no matter how specialized, that is related to a basic trade or skills.

Formal agreements are far more important today

Internal software protection programs today must rely far more heavily on formal agreements between the employer and employee than on unilaterally promulgated rules. These agreements must include adequate compensation for any rights waived, and constraints on employee mobility or use of information must be tied to the job level (i.e., you cannot make the same demands of a secretary that you make of an inventor).

The program should match the job

The key to protecting software and other assets from employee misappropriation is a formal program of education and reaffirmed understandings that starts with the job interview and runs through the entire employment period. In this way the basis of trust established as a part of and as a condition to employment can be expanded at every job review, raise, or promotion.

A Brief Note about Contracts and Lawyers

Whether written or oral, explicit or implicit, contracts are the essence of any business relationship. They define the conditions of sale,

Contracts are too important to be left to lawyers

Write them yourself, in plain English, *then* **give them to a lawyer**

the terms of employment, and the follow-on obligations of the parties.

The old saying that anyone who acts as his or her own lawyer has a fool for a client may have a corollary: Anyone who lets his or her lawyer make policy is foolhardy. Asking a lawyer to draft a set of employment or customer agreements, for example, without first establishing the policies under which you wish to do business, is a dereliction of management responsibility.

As we have noted, a comprehensive program of software protection requires a set of contractual agreements between you and your customers, agents, and employees. While these agreements cannot override applicable law, they can and should clear up all of the "grey" areas, of which there are many. These agreements need not be elaborate. In fact, the right approach is to have them drafted in plain English by the highest level of responsible management, then (and only then) have them reviewed by your attorney. If your attorney wants to add conditions, make sure you understand why. It is the lawyer's job to warn you of, and try to protect you against, every obscure condition that might arise. This will serve you well if you (1) cast out the trivial and silly, (2) insist on simplicity and clarity of language, and (3) completely understand the *business* terms represented in the contract. As Robert Townsend said in *Up the Organization,* "Beware of the lawyer who talks Middle English or statutory paragraph numbers." A good lawyer will both speak your language and welcome your management of the process.

Chapter 3 will give you a list of ideas to incorporate in your own contracts as well as a "cook book" approach to the other aspects of software protection.

3

A TEN-STEP PROGRAM FOR SOFTWARE PROTECTION

Introduction

Chapter 2 introduced the basic concepts that should underly a program of software protection. This chapter will give you the program to follow, without extensive explanation. The succeeding chapters treat each of the major topics in depth.

The recommendations in this chapter can stand alone. In other words, you need not read the next chapter on patents to know that patents are not going to help you much, but the information is there if you want to know why. Because this chapter is a summary of the recommendations found throughout the book, cross-references appear wherever appropriate.

What to Do

Decide what is important

1. *Establish priorities.* Rank the following in decreasing order of the threat posed to your business, noting whether the threat is real (i.e., known to have occurred to you or a competitor) or simply a future risk.

   a. Customer piracy, i.e., private copying of your software in harmful quantities

   b. Appropriation by competitors of the confidential designs, ideas, or implementation techniques that are embedded in your software

   c. Distribution of your software by unauthorized agents

   d. Potential employee defections to competitors or to new businesses

   Use this list to set priorities. Keep in mind that you probably will not be able to do everything and that all the recommendations that follow carry a price tag, even if only in management time and effort. For example, if the threat of private copying is not now significant, there is no reason to implement special physical and economic deterrents. Similarly, if employee defections are a real problem, you will want to concentrate on better employee relations and internal security systems for your confidential information.

Notice costs practically nothing...

But is worth a lot

2. *Give proper notice.* Everything you write, including all of your software, has an automatic copyright from the moment of creation. You can limit or lose these rights if you fail to provide notice or if you fail to use the correct format. For purposes of copyright, a work is considered "published," and thus requires notice, even if you merely lend a copy to someone else. There is *nothing* lost by giving proper notice.

For works without trade secrets

   a. If your work does *not* contain confidential information the notice should be:

   © COPYRIGHT XYZ Corp. 1985 ALL RIGHTS RESERVED.

   Note that the "c" must be in a closed circle whenever physically possible (e.g., on all external labels and printed materials).

   b. If the work *does* contain confidential information or trade secrets the notice should be:

And those with

   NOTICE: PROPRIETARY AND CONFIDENTIAL MATERIAL. DISTRIBUTION, USE, AND DISCLOSURE RESTRICTED BY LICENSE. © COPYRIGHT, XYZ Corp. 1985 ALL RIGHTS RESERVED.

Once again, the "c" must be in a closed circle whenever physically possible (e.g., on all external labels and printed materials).

Where to put it

c. Put the appropriate notice:

1) on the front and cover of all manuals. If unbound, put the notice on the frontispiece or title page;
2) on the bottom of every unbound page and on any pages a customer or agent will be permitted to copy;
3) at least on every other page of fan-folded printouts. *Modify all program maintenance and library routines to do this automatically;*
4) on the initial display for any program with visual output;
5) on all copies or derivatives of the work, e.g., on object-code listings and on read-only memory (ROM) containing the program;
6) on labels affixed to all physical media containing the materials, e.g., tape reels, floppy disks, and storage and shipping boxes.

Update your notice

d. Put the notice on immediately. Use the year of creation in the notice. If you are updating an old work, add the new date but do not remove the old one, for example:

Keep copies

© COPYRIGHT XYZ Corp. 1982, 1985

e. Keep an archival copy of each generation of a work showing the notice given.

You can repair a missing notice

f. If you have existing works that were first distributed less than five years ago but without proper notice, you can remedy the problem by (1) giving notice *now* to as many holders of the work as possible, and (2) registering the copyright as described below.

Early registration brings substantial benefits

3. *Register your copyright.* Copyright registration for software is widely misunderstood. Registration is required before any infringement suit may be brought. This can be done just before you go to court, but certain benefits, including recovery of legal fees and the availability of statutory damages, are lost if you did not register before the infringement occurred. Nonetheless, most software developers have not registered their copyrights, possibly in the mistaken belief that this cannot be done without disclosing trade secrets. It is true that registration nominally requires a deposit of the software, but there are ways to insure confidentiality:

a. If your software does *not* contain trade secrets or confidential information, simply register the source code as a literary

FORM TX

UNITED STATES COPYRIGHT OFFICE

REGISTRATION NUMBER

_____

TX   TXU

EFFECTIVE DATE OF REGISTRATION

_____

Month   Day   Year

DO NOT WRITE ABOVE THIS LINE. IF YOU NEED MORE SPACE, USE A SEPARATE CONTINUATION SHEET.

1

TITLE OF THIS WORK ▼

PREVIOUS OR ALTERNATIVE TITLES ▼

PUBLICATION AS A CONTRIBUTION If this work was published as a contribution to a periodical, serial, or collection, give information about the collective work in which the contribution appeared. **Title of Collective Work ▼**

If published in a periodical or serial give: Volume ▼	Number ▼	Issue Date ▼	On Pages ▼

2

a

NAME OF AUTHOR ▼

DATES OF BIRTH AND DEATH
Year Born ▼   Year Died ▼

Was this contribution to the work a "work made for hire"?
☐ Yes
☐ No

AUTHOR'S NATIONALITY OR DOMICILE
Name of Country
OR { Citizen of ▶ _____
    Domiciled in ▶ _____

WAS THIS AUTHOR'S CONTRIBUTION TO THE WORK
Anonymous? ☐ Yes ☐ No
Pseudonymous? ☐ Yes ☐ No
If the answer to either of these questions is "Yes," see detailed instructions.

NATURE OF AUTHORSHIP Briefly describe nature of the material created by this author in which copyright is claimed. ▼

NOTE

Under the law, the "author" of a "work made for hire" is generally the employer, not the employee (see instructions). For any part of this work that was "made for hire" check "Yes" in the space provided, give the employer (or other person for whom the work was prepared) as "Author" of that part, and leave the space for dates of birth and death blank.

b

NAME OF AUTHOR ▼

DATES OF BIRTH AND DEATH
Year Born ▼   Year Died ▼

Was this contribution to the work a "work made for hire"?
☐ Yes
☐ No

AUTHOR'S NATIONALITY OR DOMICILE
Name of country
OR { Citizen of ▶ _____
    Domiciled in ▶ _____

WAS THIS AUTHOR'S CONTRIBUTION TO THE WORK
Anonymous? ☐ Yes ☐ No
Pseudonymous? ☐ Yes ☐ No
If the answer to either of these questions is "Yes," see detailed instructions.

NATURE OF AUTHORSHIP Briefly describe nature of the material created by this author in which copyright is claimed. ▼

c

NAME OF AUTHOR ▼

DATES OF BIRTH AND DEATH
Year Born ▼   Year Died ▼

Was this contribution to the work a "work made for hire"?
☐ Yes
☐ No

AUTHOR'S NATIONALITY OR DOMICILE
Name of Country
OR { Citizen of ▶ _____
    Domiciled in ▶ _____

WAS THIS AUTHOR'S CONTRIBUTION TO THE WORK
Anonymous? ☐ Yes ☐ No
Pseudonymous? ☐ Yes ☐ No
If the answer to either of these questions is "Yes," see detailed instructions.

NATURE OF AUTHORSHIP Briefly describe nature of the material created by this author in which copyright is claimed. ▼

3

YEAR IN WHICH CREATION OF THIS WORK WAS COMPLETED This information must be given in all cases. ◀ Year

DATE AND NATION OF FIRST PUBLICATION OF THIS PARTICULAR WORK
Complete this information Month ▶ _____ Day ▶ _____ Year ▶ _____
ONLY if this work has been published.   ◀ Nation

4

See instructions before completing this space.

COPYRIGHT CLAIMANT(S) Name and address must be given even if the claimant is the same as the author given in space 2.▼

TRANSFER If the claimant(s) named here in space 4 are different from the author(s) named in space 2, give a brief statement of how the claimant(s) obtained ownership of the copyright.▼

APPLICATION RECEIVED

ONE DEPOSIT RECEIVED

TWO DEPOSITS RECEIVED

REMITTANCE NUMBER AND DATE

DO NOT WRITE HERE — OFFICE USE ONLY

MORE ON BACK ▶
• Complete all applicable spaces (numbers 5-11) on the reverse side of this page.
• See detailed instructions.
• Sign the form at line 10.

DO NOT WRITE HERE

Page 1 of_____pages

FIGURE 3.1 Form TX

EXAMINED BY

CHECKED BY

☐ CORRESPONDENCE
   Yes

☐ DEPOSIT ACCOUNT
   FUNDS USED

FORM TX

FOR
COPYRIGHT
OFFICE
USE
ONLY

DO NOT WRITE ABOVE THIS LINE. IF YOU NEED MORE SPACE, USE A SEPARATE CONTINUATION SHEET.

PREVIOUS REGISTRATION Has registration for this work, or for an earlier version of this work, already been made in the Copyright Office?
☐ Yes ☐ No   If your answer is "Yes," why is another registration being sought? (Check appropriate box) ▼
☐ This is the first published edition of a work previously registered in unpublished form.
☐ This is the first application submitted by this author as copyright claimant.
☐ This is a changed version of the work, as shown by space 6 on this application.
If your answer is "Yes," give: **Previous Registration Number** ▼   **Year of Registration** ▼

5

DERIVATIVE WORK OR COMPILATION Complete both space 6a & 6b for a derivative work; complete only 6b for a compilation.
a. Preexisting Material Identify any preexisting work or works that this work is based on or incorporates. ▼

b. Material Added to This Work Give a brief, general statement of the material that has been added to this work and in which copyright is claimed. ▼

6

See instructions
before completing
this space.

MANUFACTURERS AND LOCATIONS If this is a published work consisting preponderantly of nondramatic literary material in English, the law may require that the copies be manufactured in the United States or Canada for full protection. If so, the names of the manufacturers who performed certain processes, and the places where these processes were performed **must** be given. See instructions for details.
Names of Manufacturers ▼   **Places of Manufacture** ▼

7

REPRODUCTION FOR USE OF BLIND OR PHYSICALLY HANDICAPPED INDIVIDUALS   A signature on this form at space 10, and a check in one of the boxes here in space 8, constitutes a non-exclusive grant of permission to the Library of Congress to reproduce and distribute solely for the blind and physically handicapped and under the conditions and limitations prescribed by the regulations of the Copyright Office: (1) copies of the work identified in space 1 of this application in Braille (or similar tactile symbols); or (2) phonorecords embodying a fixation of a reading of that work; or (3) both.

a ☐ Copies and Phonorecords   b ☐ Copies Only   c ☐ Phonorecords Only

8

See instructions.

DEPOSIT ACCOUNT If the registration fee is to be charged to a Deposit Account established in the Copyright Office, give name and number of Account.
Name ▼   **Account Number** ▼

9

CORRESPONDENCE Give name and address to which correspondence about this application should be sent. Name/Address/Apt/City/State/Zip ▼

Be sure to
give your
daytime phone
◀ number.

Area Code & Telephone Number ▶

CERTIFICATION* I, the undersigned, hereby certify that I am the
                                              Check one ▶
☐ author
☐ other copyright claimant
☐ owner of exclusive right(s)
☐ authorized agent of _____
                                        Name of author or other copyright claimant, or owner of exclusive right(s) ▲

of the work identified in this application and that the statements made
by me in this application are correct to the best of my knowledge.

10

Typed or printed name and date ▼ If this is a published work, this date must be the same as or later than the date of publication given in space 3.

_____ date ▶ _____

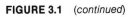 Handwritten signature (X) ▼

**MAIL
CERTIFI-
CATE TO**

Name ▼

Number/Street/Apartment Number ▼

**Certificate
will be
mailed in
window
envelope**

City/State/ZIP ▼

Have you:
• Completed all necessary spaces?
• Signed your application in space 10?
• Enclosed check or money order for $10 payable to *Register of Copyrights?*
• Enclosed your deposit material with the application and fee?

MAIL TO: Register of Copyrights, Library of Congress, Washington, D.C. 20559.

11

* 17 U.S.C. § 506(e) Any person who knowingly makes a false representation of a material fact in the application for copyright registration provided for by section 409, or in any written statement filed in connection with the application, shall be fined not more than $2,500.

☆ U.S. GOVERNMENT PRINTING OFFICE: 1982·361·278/58

Sept. 1982—600,000

FIGURE 3.1   *(continued)*

work. (Use the United States Copyright Office's Form TX. The Copyright Office provides free forms, instructions, and a "hotline" service.[4] Figure 3.1 is a sample application.)

You must do a little work if trade secrets are involved

Request secure deposit

b. If your software *does* contain trade secrets or other confidential material, first write to the Chief of the Acquisitions and Processing Division at the Copyright Office and request special relief from the deposit requirements. State that because of the confidentiality of the material you wish to be relieved of any deposit requirements but would accept a method of secure deposit, e.g., confidential examination followed by return of the source code, but with deposit of a representative sample from the work, such as a listing of the middle ten characters from each line of source code. Until enough requests of this type are received regularly by the Copyright Office they will continue to be denied on the basis of administrative burden. You have nothing to lose in making the request, however, and change is in the wind.

Do not use the "rule of doubt"

c. If your request for secure deposit is denied, *do not* deposit copies of your object code under the so-called "rule of doubt," as has been widely recommended. There is no judicial support for this point yet, but it is possible that a court could hold that deposit of your trade secrets, in any form, constitutes disclosure (and hence loss of trade secrecy).

Deposit nonconfidential segments

d. *Do* register your source code, but only after moving all of the trade secret and other confidential information to the center of the program. Specifically, organize the program so the first and last twenty-five pages of the source listing are made up of nonconfidential notes, program descriptions, constants, storage assignments, cross-references, and the like. Pad it if necessary. The Copyright Office (currently) requires only these fifty pages to satisfy its deposit requirement. It is a good idea to submit the balance of the program in sufficient detail to identify the work without disclosing it (e.g., the middle ten characters from each line of source code).

Put notice on your unpublished materials

e. Do *not* register any confidential design documents, but *do* put your copyright notice on them along with the notice of confidentiality. As unpublished works they are exempt from the deposit requirements, but notice is required to defeat a claim of "innocent" infringement.

Register all audio-visual works separately

f. If your software creates fixed images (e.g., a series of "fill-in-the-blanks" displays), or repetitive sights and sounds (e.g., video games and training programs) you should *also* register these as audio-visual works on the United States Copyright

FORM PA
UNITED STATES COPYRIGHT OFFICE

REGISTRATION NUMBER

PA   PAU

EFFECTIVE DATE OF REGISTRATION

Month	Day	Year

DO NOT WRITE ABOVE THIS LINE. IF YOU NEED MORE SPACE, USE A SEPARATE CONTINUATION SHEET.

1

TITLE OF THIS WORK ▼

PREVIOUS OR ALTERNATIVE TITLES ▼

NATURE OF THIS WORK ▼ See instructions

2

a

NAME OF AUTHOR ▼

DATES OF BIRTH AND DEATH
Year Born ▼   Year Died ▼

Was this contribution to the work a "work made for hire"?
☐ Yes
☐ No

AUTHOR'S NATIONALITY OR DOMICILE
Name of Country
OR { Citizen of ▶_____
     Domiciled in ▶_____

WAS THIS AUTHOR'S CONTRIBUTION TO THE WORK
Anonymous? ☐ Yes ☐ No
Pseudonymous? ☐ Yes ☐ No

If the answer to either of these questions is "Yes," see detailed instructions.

NOTE
Under the law, the "author" of a "work made for hire" is generally the employer, not the employee (see instructions). For any part of this work that was "made for hire" check "Yes" in the space provided, give the employer (or other person for whom the work was prepared) as "Author" of that part, and leave the space for dates of birth and death blank.

NATURE OF AUTHORSHIP Briefly describe nature of the material created by this author in which copyright is claimed. ▼

b

NAME OF AUTHOR ▼

DATES OF BIRTH AND DEATH
Year Born ▼   Year Died ▼

Was this contribution to the work a "work made for hire"?
☐ Yes
☐ No

AUTHOR'S NATIONALITY OR DOMICILE
Name of country
OR { Citizen of ▶_____
     Domiciled in ▶_____

WAS THIS AUTHOR'S CONTRIBUTION TO THE WORK
Anonymous? ☐ Yes ☐ No
Pseudonymous? ☐ Yes ☐ No

If the answer to either of these questions is "Yes," see detailed instructions.

NATURE OF AUTHORSHIP Briefly describe nature of the material created by this author in which copyright is claimed. ▼

c

NAME OF AUTHOR ▼

DATES OF BIRTH AND DEATH
Year Born ▼   Year Died ▼

Was this contribution to the work a "work made for hire"?
☐ Yes
☐ No

AUTHOR'S NATIONALITY OR DOMICILE
Name of Country
OR { Citizen of ▶_____
     Domiciled in ▶_____

WAS THIS AUTHOR'S CONTRIBUTION TO THE WORK
Anonymous? ☐ Yes ☐ No
Pseudonymous? ☐ Yes ☐ No

If the answer to either of these questions is "Yes," see detailed instructions.

NATURE OF AUTHORSHIP Briefly describe nature of the material created by this author in which copyright is claimed. ▼

3

YEAR IN WHICH CREATION OF THIS WORK WAS COMPLETED This information must be given in all cases.
◀ Year

DATE AND NATION OF FIRST PUBLICATION OF THIS PARTICULAR WORK
Complete this information ONLY if this work has been published.
Month ▶ _____ Day ▶ _____ Year ▶ _____
◀ Nation

4

COPYRIGHT CLAIMANT(S) Name and address must be given even if the claimant is the same as the author given in space 2.▼

See instructions before completing this space.

TRANSFER If the claimant(s) named here in space 4 are different from the author(s) named in space 2, give a brief statement of how the claimant(s) obtained ownership of the copyright.▼

APPLICATION RECEIVED

ONE DEPOSIT RECEIVED

TWO DEPOSITS RECEIVED

REMITTANCE NUMBER AND DATE

DO NOT WRITE HERE OFFICE USE ONLY

MORE ON BACK ▶
• Complete all applicable spaces (numbers 5-9) on the reverse side of this page.
• See detailed instructions.
• Sign the form at line 8.

DO NOT WRITE HERE

Page 1 of _____ pages

FIGURE 3.2 Form PA

DO NOT WRITE ABOVE THIS LINE. IF YOU NEED MORE SPACE, USE A SEPARATE CONTINUATION SHEET.

PREVIOUS REGISTRATION Has registration for this work, or for an earlier version of this work, already been made in the Copyright Office?

☐ **Yes** ☐ **No** If your answer is "Yes," why is another registration being sought? (Check appropriate box) ▼

☐ This is the first published edition of a work previously registered in unpublished form.

☐ This is the first application submitted by this author as copyright claimant.

☐ This is a changed version of the work, as shown by space 6 on this application.

If your answer is "Yes," give: **Previous Registration Number ▼**   **Year of Registration ▼**

5

DERIVATIVE WORK OR COMPILATION Complete both space 6a & 6b for a derivative work; complete only 6b for a compilation.

a. Preexisting Material Identify any preexisting work or works that this work is based on or incorporates. ▼

b. Material Added to This Work Give a brief, general statement of the material that has been added to this work and in which copyright is claimed.▼

6

See instructions
before completing
this space.

DEPOSIT ACCOUNT If the registration fee is to be charged to a Deposit Account established in the Copyright Office, give name and number of Account.

Name ▼   **Account Number ▼**

7

CORRESPONDENCE Give name and address to which correspondence about this application should be sent. Name/Address/Apt/City/State/Zip ▼

Area Code & Telephone Number ▶

Be sure to
give your
daytime phone
◀ number.

CERTIFICATION* I, the undersigned, hereby certify that I am the

Check only one ▼

☐ author

☐ other copyright claimant

☐ owner of exclusive right(s)

☐ authorized agent of_____
           Name of author or other copyright claimant, or owner of exclusive right(s) ▲

8

of the work identified in this application and that the statements made
by me in this application are correct to the best of my knowledge.

Typed or printed name and date ▼ If this is a published work, this date must be the same as or later than the date of publication given in space 3.

_____ date ▶ _____

 **Handwritten signature (X) ▼**

* 17 U.S.C. § 506(e) Any person who knowingly makes a false representation of a material fact in the application for copyright registration provided for by section 409, or in any written statement filed in connection with the application, shall be fined not more than $2.500.

⋆ U.S. GOVERNMENT PRINTING OFFICE: 1983—381-278/505

Sept. 1983—100,000

FIGURE 3.2 *(continued)*

Office's Form PA, as shown in Fig. 3.2. This can be done by depositing a video tape of the images (and sounds, if applicable).

**Register with the
customs service**

g. If imported copies of your software are a real or possible problem, also register your copyright with the U.S. Customs Office in Washington. Customs can seize pirated works at their port of entry.

**You have a trade
secret if . . .**

4. *Protect your confidential information.* Confidential information is a broad term that includes trade secrets and other materials. Protecting this information requires advance notice of confidentiality, a basis of trust between the parties, and physical security. Failure to reach an agreement of trust is the most common basis for loss of secrecy and related conflicts. The following is especially important, as a single disclosure can forever invalidate a claim of trade secrecy:

**You give
advance notice,**

a. Establish formal labeling procedures.
   1) Mark materials according to their level of confidentiality, e.g., "company confidential" or "secret."
   2) Do not stamp everything indiscriminately; itemize materials to be protected by class and make labeling a formalized process.

**Create an environment
of security,**

b. Create security measures to match the levels of confidentiality.
   1) Confidential materials widely distributed within the organization (e.g., customer lists) should not be subject to the same level of protection as more restricted materials (e.g., design documents). The former can be protected with written procedures prohibiting disclosure to outsiders and specifying accepted disposal techniques.
   2) More sensitive materials, especially documents containing very valuable trade secrets, require more extensive security measures (e.g., formal logging of access, prohibitions on copying, and physical security).

**. . . Like restricted
access,**

   3) Be sure to restrict access to those with a "need to know." Do not permit anyone with general access to the company's computers, for example, to then have automatic access to trade secrets (e.g., source code).
   4) Keep detailed records of copies produced and distributed. Number each copy if possible.
   5) Post security procedures where they can be seen.
   6) Establish a formal review procedure to examine all materials for the presence of confidential and trade secret information prior to any distribution or publication.

Nondisclosure agreements,

c. Obtain nondisclosure agreements from all prospects, customers, agents, and employees *before* you permit any access to confidential materials.
   1) Always use written agreements.
   2) To avoid a prolonged legal process that could cost sales, arm your sales representatives with simple "postcard" agreements that simply commit the prospect to a confidential relationship.

Employment terms . . .

   3) In any contracts with agents and customers make sure your agent or customer is responsible for any downstream disclosures made by its agents or employees.
   4) Make acceptance of your rights in confidential materials a precondition of employment and of promotions; see item 6 below.

d. Put a few "nonsense" instructions in your programs (and nonexistent customers on your customer lists). This will give you a "smoking gun" in the case of outright theft.

. . . And a basis of trust

Recognize rights of your employees

5. *Establish a basis of trust with your employees.* Employees represent the single most important consideration in any intangible asset protection program. Most trade secrecy and unfair competition cases involve ex-employees, not customers or prospects. A lack of clear understanding of the employer's and the employee's rights and obligations is the most common culprit. Also, courts and legislatures have been changing the rules. Today, a formal agreement between the parties is essential if trade secrets, confidential information, or proprietary inventions are involved. These agreements should be in writing and should reflect some balance between the competing interests of the parties. Employers who recognize and respect the rights of their employees will have a far better chance of enforcing their own claims or avoiding conflicts altogether. Any threat to a company's well-being affects its employees. Your employees are intelligent enough to grasp the need to protect *their* livelihoods. As Alfred P. Sloan said, "It is better to appeal to the intelligence of a man than to issue orders."

An employee handbook works

a. Create a Handbook of Business Conduct and Practices. Include clear statements on the ownership of trade secrets, inventions, and confidential information. Reference or include specific procedures to be followed in dealing with these materials. Spell out prohibited practices.

. . . If it is a basis of employment

b. Make the Handbook a condition of employment. Reference its terms in every application for employment. Make all promotions and raises subject to reconfirmation of its terms.

**But don't usurp
legitimate rights**

c. *Do not:*
1) attempt to transfer blanket rights to the company; you will alienate employees and may weaken your legitimate claims;
2) claim ownership to inventions or writings made by the employee on his or her own time, without company resources, which are unrelated to the employee's job assignment;
3) claim as your own any trade secrets brought to the job by the employee; these should be itemized and excluded as part of the employment process;

**Or place unilateral
restrictions on
future employment**

4) with very few exceptions (see item d below), try to place restrictions on the employee's future employment rights or rights to compete with you, *except* to prohibit the use of your confidential information;
5) attempt to claim general industry knowledge (i.e., the same information that would be provided in competitive employment) as a trade secret, no matter how specialized.

d. There are guidelines you should follow for those employees who are hired to develop or use trade secrets.

**For a few key
employees contracts
are appropriate**

1) If they are key employees, supplement the Handbook and standard employment agreement with individualized employment contracts. As with the Handbook, acceptance should be a precondition of employment or promotion.
2) Recognizing that they are difficult or impossible to enforce, you may nonetheless want to include a specific, severable, noncompete clause in a supplemental employment contract. If you do, limit it to a specific narrow list of competitors in a clearly defined geographic area and for a short time period.

**Team efforts are more
easily protected**

3) Beware of individual inventors; if you contribute little or nothing to their work they may have a right to use what they develop in subsequent employment. Log all contributions to a team effort. Record all disclosure of preexisting trade secrets and other uses of company facilities in developing new products (e.g., computer time).

Train, train, . . .

4) Conduct regular training sessions, reinforce the rationale for the company's procedures and policies, and encourage debate. Consider making employee awards for suggestions on improved security procedures.
5) Make knowledge of and adherence to security procedures a formal part of every employment review, especially for managers; add training in same to all management training programs.

Don't try to make a private exchange out of a retail sale . . . you'll lose

6. *Use the right form of transaction.* This step sounds obvious, but it is not. Whether you own or can control the rights to your software is in large measure a question determined by the form of the transaction used to pass that software on to agents, distributors, dealers, and customers.

   a. If you are selling products through retail outlets, as most microcomputer software vendors do, there is no way to avoid the Uniform Commercial Code (UCC), which applies in nearly every state. So-called "license agreements," which attempt to convert the transaction from the "sale of goods" regulated by the UCC into a transfer of intangible rights (not regulated by the UCC), have not yet been legally tested, but are far more likely to fail a court challenge than not. The prudent vendor selling software products through retail outlets will operate as if the Uniform Commercial Code applies and structure the transaction accordingly.

      1) Don't count on having any enforceable agreements with the end user; rather, look to the force of applicable law to protect your interests (most notably, from a software protection standpoint, copyright).

A limited warranty (and maybe a right of return) beats an outright disclaimer

      2) Include an explicit limited warranty with the product rather than disclaiming all warranties. You might, for example, offer the buyer a refund during a limited time period should the product fail to perform as documented. At the same time, you can prominently disclaim all other warranties and liabilities (especially implied warranties and consequential damages). The advantage of this approach is that the buyer is given a reasonable opportunity to reject the product and, in the absence of rejection, acceptance can be argued.

Try to create a post-sale relationship

      3) Establish a post-sale contractual relationship with the customer to replace all other obligations. This can be done by including an agreement with each product which, if accepted and returned, will provide additional services (e.g., extended support, upgrades, additional backup copies, etc.) but under new terms and conditions. As your exposure to consequential damages and implied warranties is potentially huge, it is worth making this offer hard for the ordinary user to refuse.

Safeguard your authority

      4) Be sure to limit the authority of any dealers, agents, or distributors to act in your behalf. A suggestion by your agent that a product will produce a specific benefit may turn into your obligation, regardless of your disclaimers.

Be reasonable

    5) It is *not* reasonable to try and restrain the customers' legitimate rights, e.g., to make backup copies or resell the product. This topic is further discussed in item 8 below.

  b. If the original transaction is between you and the end user, without any intermediary, take precautionary measures.

Never transfer ownership

    1) Never "sell" the software to the customer. Avoid any language that implies anything more than the transfer of a right to use a proprietary process, confidential information, and trade secrets.

    2) Make sure the contract specifies that all rights, title, and interest in the underlying software remain yours.

    3) Make your disclosure of trade secrets and/or confidential information part of the contractual "consideration."

    4) Limit the customers' rights to use the materials disclosed and transferred to those specified in your documentation.

If possible, deal with the customer, not an intermediary

  c. When an intermediary must be involved, attempt to keep a direct relationship with the end user. Avoid "dealers" or "distributors" (who buy and then resell) whenever possible. These relationships are highly unsuitable to the transfer of intangible rights and can create *huge* problems of enforcement, especially outside of the United States. It is always preferable to end up in a direct relationship with the ultimate customer, even if this means granting some extra authority to the agent who operates on your behalf. This subject is covered in item 9 below.

7. *Audit and test the system.* No passive scheme to protect intangible assets will work. One of the best ways to insure *active* compliance and participation is to have a formal audit program.

Confirm every contract

  a. Confirming the terms of a contract is good practice, unrelated to software protection. For example, there have been numerous cases of fraud involving falsified sales by sales personnel. A simple but effective technique used by many companies to catch such problems quickly is to have a central contract administrator send a confirming copy of the sales documents, along with a "thank you for the business" letter, to a senior executive of the customer. If confidentiality provisions are involved, this letter can also contain a reminder of any such obligations (e.g., "As you have agreed to take special steps in protecting our confidential information, we would welcome any requests for advice in this area").

Randomly audit shipments

  b. If software is provided subject to a nondisclosure agreement, randomly audit actual shipments to insure that such documents were indeed on file before delivery. Simultaneously confirm that any confidential material provided to prospects was returned if the transaction was never completed.

Drop in on your employees

c. "Management by Walking Around" can be a very effective tool. Random inspections of company premises should be an assigned task for all managers; supply a checklist.
   1) Note any confidential materials left in open areas.
   2) Insure that discarded confidential materials do not end up in the wrong place, e.g., as packing paper for shipments.
   3) Check the physical security systems, e.g., doors and cabinets are closed and locked when not in use.

d. Poll your employees. This can simultaneously educate and uncover bad practices. Look for problems, not victims.

Can you break your own systems?

e. Check the security systems. Ask a clever employee to break in to a supposedly secure on-line database and get a source program listing, for example. Hire a professional to try to talk his or her way into restricted buildings or areas (but provide an explanatory letter in case your security system works!).

Audit your personnel procedures

f. Randomly check personnel files to insure that:
   1) the terms of employment, as spelled out in your Handbook, were agreed to as a precondition of employment (i.e., there is a signed copy of an application for employment with an explicit reference to these terms);
   2) there is a formal employee reaffirmation of these terms on each status-change form associated with a raise or promotion;
   3) acknowledgments are on file from all ex-employees concerning confidential information and materials.

Are you encouraging theft?

8. *Reexamine and rebalance the economic incentives to steal.* This is possibly the most important step. If you are providing customers, employees, or agents with an overwhelming incentive to steal, some will. The best way to begin this analysis is to look at the incentives from the outside-in, i.e., why would someone choose to steal rather than deal honestly?

a. If customers are making illicit copies of your software, greed may not be the primary motive. Do you have a flexible backup policy, for example? One very successful microcomputer software product has been widely duplicated by legitimate buyers using unauthorized means, primarily because the vendor limits the user to a single backup copy that will operate only if the original copy is still at least partially usable. Fearing loss, fire, hot coffee, etc., many buyers have turned to special programs that will copy a vendor's "protected" disks. Forcing the user to employ the tools of a thief to do perfectly legal copying reduces the barriers to illegitimate copying.

Greed (yours) may be the problem

b. Frequently, the incentive to steal is indeed greed, but surprisingly it is the buyer's perception of the vendor's greed. Failure of a software vendor to offer a multisite or multimachine licensing agreement, for example, is frequently cited as justification for illegitimate copying.

    1) "We're just using the second copy for educational purposes."

    2) "Why should we pay for two copies when our total usage is only several hours a week?"

Don't provide easy excuses

    3) "I need a copy at home at night. It's silly to have to pay for two copies when only one is ever in use at the same time."

    4) "Do you realize what 400 copies would cost? It doesn't cost the vendor one penny more for us to use 400 copies than it would if we just had one."

Flexibility can buy a lot

While each and every one of these self-justifying explanations is wrong, there is an important message here. Both parties may have lost because of the vendor's pricing and distribution policies. Had the vendor offered a corporate license (e.g., up to x local copies for a fixed fee and discounts to second-site users), the vendor could have received more total compensation, extended the product's legitimate usage, improved cash flow by earning fees upfront, added contractual guarantees that would have been otherwise unobtainable, improved customer relations, and gained access to an invaluable new pool of user/prospects. The customer would have gained as well, spending more in total but less per copy, gaining additional access to vendor services, and discouraging illegal and unethical copying.

Perception can become reality

c. Perceptions frequently become reality. Vendor services are often ascribed monetary values that are unrelated to their costs. Judicious use of these services can tip the balance from an incentive to steal to an incentive to become or remain a legitimate user. Packaging is the key. If more perceived value can be created for services available only to legitimate customers, the price at which theft becomes an economically attractive option rises. Here are a few to consider:

    1) "hot line" access to support personnel;

    2) regular documentation updates;

    3) newsletters and product bulletins (e.g., containing usage tips, "work arounds" for known problems, etc.);

    4) product update services (i.e., news of and easy access to new releases);

    5) membership in a user's group;

    6) discounts on future purchases.

Physical constraints just raise the ante

...But don't kill off your customers

d. Use physical barriers to raise the stakes for a thief. As previously noted, there is no physical protection scheme that cannot be broken; it is merely a question of money and time. Encryption, software locks, and hardware keys are simply different levels of barrier to theft (and, in some cases, to legitimate use). Use of these techniques should be balanced by the need. Many vendors have discovered that their paranoia about anticipated thievery has cost them legitimate customers who will not put up with overly burdensome usage constraints. Conversely, there are simple barriers to thievery that place virtually no burdens on the user, yet these barriers are routinely overlooked.

Hardware barriers...

1) Hardware protections (e.g., distributing the software only in ROM or supplying a hardware "key" that is checked by an encryptified part of the program) raise the greatest barriers to theft, and cost the most. These forms of protection are only justified for the extreme ends of the spectrum (low volume but high cost, or very low cost but high volume software). Even then, there are devices on the market designed to capture a program from the memory of a computer while it is running (after the security checks have been passed), and thus will defeat most such schemes.

Software barriers...

2) Software barriers to copying are the easiest to use but they are also the easiest to defeat and are the most problematic for the legitimate user. The most common method used involves writing some of the software on an area of the distribution disk that is not accessed by other programs, most notably the normal copy routines. The result is that an entire industry has grown up selling programs that will copy anything, even disks that appear to contain errors (and programs that will copy protected programs!).

And natural barriers

3) The simplest barriers are sometimes the most effective, especially for medium-priced products (e.g., documentation which, because of its color, shape, or packaging, is difficult or expensive to copy).

Simple password schemes usually fail

4) In-house protections against unauthorized access are frequently ignored or trivial. Simple passwords are the most common access protection scheme used for on-line sytems. Passwords are frequently widely known or recorded in plain view near the terminals. Recently, young hobbyists broke into several extremely sensitive systems by randomly trying phone numbers in search of the carrier frequencies characteristic of computer traffic and then keying commonly used passwords (i.e., "help," "service,"

girls' names, etc.). Their rate of success was astounding.

- [ ] Organize passwords by class of access and "need to know." Do not make rank or prior access rights a criteria for access; every piece of sensitive on-line information should have an identified list of legitimate accessors.

... But dynamic systems do work

- [ ] Create a dynamic mechanism, beyond passwords, for identifying the user. One excellent scheme is to build a confidential profile of each user by having the individual enter such obscure information as mother's maiden name, wedding anniversary, birthdays, and the like. After a conventional password test, a randomly selected question from the profile can be asked (e.g., "Please enter your oldest child's birthday"). Such systems are very hard for all but the most serious thief to defeat, yet they pose minimal constraints on the user.

Act quickly

d. Be prepared to move quickly and show little mercy if, despite your best efforts, a customer, agent, or employee decides to break his or her relationship of trust with you. Letting the world know that you are prepared to use every means to protect your rights is an excellent way to avoid conflicts in the first place. See item 10, below.

Third parties can become competitors

9. *Deal intelligently with third parties.* It is bad enough to have a new competitor. It is worse to have a new competitor who is using your products, customer lists, or other assets to compete. The worst of all, however, is to have a new competitor operate unfairly, with your financing. It is suprising how often this happens. A company invests in a new market by assigning an agent, dealer, or representative to cover a territory. When the investment begins to reap rewards the company discovers that the agent has negotiated a more lucrative deal with a competitor or has decided to compete directly. Alternatively, a company hires an outside contractor to develop part or all of a new product. Subsequently, the company finds a similar product in the marketplace, developed by, and possibly marketed by, guess who.

Especially if they act as your customer versus your agent

Dealers and distributors may have local rights

The problem is complicated when the third party is an independent agent or contractor. Local laws may prohibit contract exclusivity, termination without arbitration, and even direct dealings with the agent's or distributor's customers. In foreign territories, special legislation to protect against "market exploitation" may preclude replacing a local representative, even for nonperformance. In France, for example, it is a violation of law to bypass the distributor and directly service or sell to accounts that were established by a local firm, without its agreement, even if the distribution agreement has been terminated for cause.

The problem posed by new laws and court rulings is not only a foreign one, however. Several states have passed "dealer protection acts" and federal legislation has been introduced in each of the last two congressional sessions to regulate the relationships between producers and their dealers. The intent of these laws is to give independent dealers more rights to the markets they serve and to subject any termination or change in terms to statutory procedures and judicial review. Although initiated by hard-goods dealer associations (notably auto dealers), the legislation does not make distinctions between products and services or between local and foreign markets.

Clarity is the key

In dealing with third parties the critical needs are a business relationship that eliminates rather than creates conflict and one that anticipates local conditions. Clarity is the key. Silence on key issues (e.g., ownership or termination procedures) will insure conflict. Here are some key items:

Identify 'works for hire'

a. There are guidelines to follow when dealing with independent contractors.

  1) Make sure that the work performed by them for you is a "work for hire" as specified in the Copyright Act. This gives you certain rights in the copyrights that might otherwise be open to question.

Keep title

  2) State clearly in your agreement that any rights, title, and interest in copyrights, trade secrets, products, and supporting materials developed by the third party belong to you.

Guarantee confidence

  3) Get explicit agreement that any confidential materials, either provided by you or developed by the contractor, will be maintained in confidence and adequately protected.

and no competition

  4) Unlike employees, independent contractors can be held to noncompete agreements—include one if appropriate.

Spell out . . .

b. There are procedures for local dealers who remarket your products at retail.

  1) Treat the dealer as your customer and the end user as the dealer's customer. Any attempts to change this natural order will weaken your relationship with the dealer while failing to bind the ultimate customer.

Terms,

  2) Make it clear that the dealer is an independent contractor and not your legal agent or representative.

Territories,

  3) Specify an exclusive or nonexclusive territory. If the territory is exclusive, be sure to include performance conditions under which exclusivity would end.

Rights,

4) If the dealer will have any rights to make copies, a right reserved to you by copyright, spell them out.

5) Limit the dealer's rights to use trademarks, your name, etc.

And termination procedures

6) Specify termination procedures, such as:
   - [ ] natural term of agreement, renewal, and notice of nonrenewal;
   - [ ] basis for termination prior to expiration (i.e., responsibilities);
   - [ ] surviving obligations (e.g., confidentiality);
   - [ ] repurchase of dealer inventory;
   - [ ] transfer of records and accounts.

7) Retain the right to change and discontinue products.

c. Follow certain criteria if you license your software to the end user.

1) The third party representing you should be an agent, not a dealer or distributor, as sales and service agents have no implied rights of ownership in the products.

Use standard form contracts

2) The contract offered by the agent should be between *you* and the customer, not the agent and the customer, as you will want a one-on-one relationship with the end user.

3) If either because time delays in contract execution would jeopardize sales or because the contracts must be in a local language, grant the agent a limited power to sign *your* standard-form agreements (and *only* standard-form agreements) on your behalf but subject to credit criteria, etc.

4) If the agent must establish a relationship with the customer as well (e.g., for follow-on services), either make this a separate agreement between the agent and the customer or make the license agreement three-way, i.e., in one agreement:
   - [ ] license the customer to use your software;
   - [ ] transfer your service obligations to the agent;
   - [ ] if the agent will have any rights to use or to make copies of confidential information make sure that the terms of use and protection mechanisms are specified.

An agency relationship has significant benefits

Note that this type of relationship will preclude subsequent claims by the agent on your customer base, establish a direct legal (and psychological) link between you and the ultimate customer, insure that the terms of business are those that you specify, and ease any transitions that might subsequently be required (e.g., to a new agent or to direct representation).

Fight if you must

10. *Be prepared to fight.* No one wins in a court battle. This fact can lead to a "it's not worth fighting" attitude, which in turn can invite challenges. A willingness to move swiftly and with every re-

source is your best defense against a court battle, but you may have to do so once to let the world know that you are not a push-over.

If you are well prepared and move swiftly you may be able to get a quick victory without the pain of protracted litigation. More and more often we see headlines like "International Business Machines Corp. filed and settled a suit against Gartner Group..." (*Wall Street Journal*, Dec. 5, 1983). In this example, as in others, the defendant agreed to settle the suit without admitting guilt, while guaranteeing to return and not make use of any trade secret information it might have. Preparedness, an apparently strong case, and a willingness to slug it out can lead to a quick and complete resolution of the dispute.

Willingness to do battle will increase the odds that you can settle on your terms

Speed is of the essence because your new adversary's investments, recruiting, and other business commitments will be harder to reverse as time passes, increasing the incentives to do battle rather than capitulate. Have a hypothetical action plan prepared for each possibility *in advance* so you can move swiftly. Delay or uncertainty will embolden your opponent, encourage others to follow suit, and decrease your chances for ultimate victory in or out of court. Conversely, swift action properly clothed in moral indignation will let everyone know that you will not be a push-over, may cause a reexamination or adjustment in plans by your new adversary, could lead to rapid settlement, and will certainly send a powerful message to others watching from the sidelines.

Prepare hypothetical war plans

Once you are convinced that there is no other course of action and that you have a winnable case, use every weapon at your disposal, one by one.

Take every step...

a. First seek a temporary injunction, pending trial, restraining the use of the misappropriated trade secrets and copyrights.

Injunction,

b. File a civil suit in U.S. District Court claiming, if applicable:
1) copyright infringement (note that up to $50,000 in statutory damages may be available to you even if you cannot prove actual losses);
2) unfair competition under state and federal law;
3) misappropriation of trade secrets under state law;
4) breach of contract.

Civil suit,

c. If you have not settled at this point, there are several steps you can take.
1) Ask the local district attorney to bring criminal charges for theft and ask a federal prosecutor to file criminal charges under the Copyright Act. Current criminal penalties under the Copyright Act provide for up to $10,000 in fines per infringement and up to one year in jail.

Criminal charges,

Public opinion,

2) Also, if you are a government contractor or if software subject to government export license is involved, ask the FBI to investigate the possibility of other federal violations.

3) Take your case to the press before the story is written by others. Get good legal advice first, but don't be afraid to use words that express moral outrage (e.g., "We believe valuable property has been stolen and will be used unfairly against us. We will use every means at our disposal to protect our employees, customers, and shareholders").

Employee support

4) Keep your employees informed. Treat them as allies. Make sure they know that they are among the victimized, and that your efforts are to protect their interests as well.

Plan to settle . . . there is no such thing as total victory

Once the battle has commenced it is considered by many a weakness to seek anything but total victory. Don't fall into this trap. After each step you should let the other side know that you are willing to settle. Instruct your attorneys to seek a negotiating forum at every chance. (While your attorneys are in court asking for your temporary injunction they can let the other side's attorneys know that the next step will be to file for damages and criminal sanctions, but that you are willing to negotiate.) Move deliberately and let the other side know each step in advance, always with an offer to negotiate. Always supply an escape route, e.g., a willingness to accept guarantees and return of materials without requiring admissions of guilt, perhaps even a willingness to license the technology under acceptable terms (this can bring valuable market information along with royalties).

Make the most of your victory. Publicize it and let the world know that you'll do it again if required.

4 EVERYTHING YOU NEED TO KNOW ABOUT PATENTS... AND MORE

What You Need to Know

Software may someday be clearly patentable

The U.S. Supreme Court may one day uphold a patent for plain and unadorned computer software. Perhaps you will be immortalized by having it be your case. In fact, if your software can meet several simple tests, the climate is right for such a challenge. Unfortunately (and to me most instructive), no software or software-related patent application that has met these simple tests has yet reached the Supreme Court. This is because most software is not patentable per se, rather than a result of the perversity of the courts.

What is a patent?

A patent grants the owner complete control over the use of the patented invention for seventeen years. During that period, a patent grants the holder "...the right to exclude others from making, using, or selling the invention throughout the United States...." Since 1793, patentable items have included inventions or discoveries consisting of "any new and useful art, machine, manufacture, or composition of matter, or any new or useful improvement thereof."[5]

Patents can include "anything under the sun"

In 1952 Congress substituted the word *process* for *art,* and the Committee Reports accompanying this revision tell us that Congress intended patentable subject matter to "include anything under the sun that is made by man."[6] This language would certainly *seem* to include software.

Processes are subject to patent

The judicial interpretation of the law evolves slowly, however. Processes had been ruled appropriate for patents by the Supreme Court as early as 1853,[7] but in 1876 a process was further defined as ". . . a mode of treatment of certain materials to provide a given result. It is an act, or a series of acts, performed upon the subject matter to be *transformed and reduced to a different state or thing*"[8] (emphasis mine). This definition permitted chemical, but not other, processes to be patented.

But it is unclear if processes that don't transform matter are included

The 1952 change in the law and several cases decided by the Court of Customs and Patent Appeals would suggest that processes that do not involve a physical transformation are now suitable subject matter for patent, but this issue has never been directly addressed by the Supreme Court.

The Supreme Court has ducked the central issue

In the cases decided by the Supreme Court to date, the question of software patentability has been both avoidable and avoided. The Court seems to have been saying, "This is a big issue. We will confront it when we must, but fortunately in this case we don't have to." The Court *has* decided some of the narrower issues, such as whether the presence of software in a patent application in and of itself is reason for rejection (it isn't), and whether laws of nature, mathematical equations, physical phenomena, or abstract ideas are patentable (they aren't).[9] In most cases, however, the Court has simply rejected the claim because the conventional tests were not met, or has sent the case back to a lower court for procedural reasons.

Even if the courts eventually honor the 1952 wish of Congress and permit all processes to be patented, including pure software, the traditional tests for patentability will still apply. Let's examine them.

The Tests

Novel, unique, useful, nonobvious and not a formula or law of nature

Your invention (software) must be novel, unique, useful, nonobvious, and it must advance the prior art. It cannot merely capture a mathematical formula, abstract idea, or method of calculation. It can *embody* a mathematical formula or method of calculation, but the invention *as a whole* must perform a function that the patent laws were designed to protect. Even if you can patent your invention, however, this will not grant you a statutory monopoly (i.e., a patent) on any part of your invention that is an algorithm, mathematical formula, method of calculation, or law of nature. As an example, you could not patent double-entry bookkeeping, $e = mc^2$, or a method for solving simultaneous linear equations.

Which leaves out most software

Because most software is a rework of an existing process

Where does this leave your new software?—probably unpatentable, even in the most favorable judicial climate. Most software is developed to reimplement an existing process for the manipulation or presentation of data. The most successful software product now on sale for large central computers, for example, performs general accounting functions, while the most successful microcomputer package provides an electronic "spread sheet." Each is the reimplementation of a formerly manual process using clever, but certainly not new or unique, techniques.

Most software is obvious or simply executes an algorithm

The patent law also provides that "a patent may not be obtained . . . if the difference between the initial subject matter sought to be patented and the prior art are such that the subject matter as a whole would have been obvious at the time the invention was made to a person having ordinary skill in the art to which the subject matter pertains . . . ." Restated, if another software developer with no special skills could have invented what you seek to patent, you had best forget it. It would appear that none of the thousands of existing programs designed to perform payroll, accounting, or other general business functions would have passed this test for obviousness. New techniques for manipulating or storing data might pass the obviousness test only to be deemed an algorithm or mental process.

Means of calculation aren't patentable

As an example, let us presume that you invented a new method for solving a series of simultaneous linear equations and wrote a program to implement it. The program would be unpatentable not because it was a program but because it was merely a method of calculation. Suppose additionally that you wrote a program to do double-entry bookkeeping using a digital computer's unique capabilities. Your patent claim would almost certainly fail the test of obviousness.

Software _could_ pass the tests

Suppose, however, that you invent some software that directs a computer to perform some new and unique function (e.g., sorting data in a process that makes unique use of the computer). If the method you use is nonobvious, novel, not merely an algorithm for moving the data, and new, you should get your patent, even if you use a mathematical formula or two incidentally in your program. Your patent will not preclude others from using a digital computer to sort data, however, nor will it preclude others from using the algorithms and formulas you included. As your invention must be registered within one year after it is first "described in a printed publication . . . or on sale . . . ,"[10] anyone who wishes to compete will have early access to the designs and ideas as well. This leads us to the question of what has been gained and what has been lost in seeking a patent.

Should You Apply for a Patent?

No; it's risky . . .

Takes too long . . .

Unless your software is part of a larger invention, you almost certainly should not apply for a patent. You have a lot to lose and almost nothing to gain. Despite the rational conclusion that patents *should* apply to pure software, there is too much risk involved for a prudent businessman to take. If you indeed do have that theoretically patentable piece of software, an unlikely event, you will face huge expenses over many years before you know for sure that you have a valid patent. Once you do have a patent, be prepared for more expense in attempting to enforce it.

Is too expensive . . .

And patents are too hard to enforce

And there are no criminal sanctions

When and if either the legislature or the courts makes patents a viable mechanism for the protection of software, most software developers will continue to use other means of protection. Patents are expensive, take several years to get, and are largely unenforceable. Historically, nearly 70 percent of all patent infringement suits are settled in favor of the alleged infringer. As the patent process requires complete disclosure, and therefore a waiver of trade secret protections, these odds seem formidable. Even if you *can* enforce your patent, the law includes no criminal sanctions for infringement; it merely provides you with a statutory basis to seek an injunction and damages. Also, many countries prohibit software patents as a matter of law,[11] hence a patent granted in the United States would have limited value in a worldwide market.

In summary, "beat me" said the masochist (patentor); "no," said the sadist (courts)

In summary, as we know them today, patents have limited value in the protection of software. For the vast majority of software developers whose craft involves the reimplementation of obvious or long-established procedures in new and clever ways, patents are of academic interest only. If you still want to proceed with your patent application, however, there is even more you should know.

. . . Even More about Patents

If you *still* want to go ahead, your first step will bring a hostile response

Patents are issued by the U.S. Patent and Trademark Office (PTO) or its foreign equivalent. Historically, the Patent Office has been opposed to patents for software on both theoretical and practical grounds, most notably due to the huge increase in its work load

Denials by the Patent Office can be appealed; first to the Patent Office's own appeals board, and then to a special court

that could result. If your claim is denied by the PTO, your appeal will be heard first by the PTO's Board of Appeals and then by a special court, the U.S. Court of Customs and Patent Appeals (CCPA). The CCPA has a history of supporting software patents. The Supreme Court can review decisions of the CCPA on request of (usually) the Patent Office, who petitions the high Court for a "writ of Certiorari" when they don't like a CCPA decision. As noted earlier, in all of the cases to date the Supreme Court has avoided the central issue of software's patentability while evincing a far less liberal view than the lower court on the conventional patentability tests and procedural issues.

The Patent Office was more positive once

The Patent Office was not always hostile to software patents. In the late 1960s and early 1970s hundreds of software patents were issued. Then, as a result of higher court decisions and a mounting work load, its position changed. At the time of the Diehr case,[12] the Patent Office referred to over 3000 pending applications that could involve software issues, a potentially crushing load.

Be cautious of early precedents; the rules keep changing

Over the past fifteen years the Patent Office, CCPA, and Supreme Court *have* resolved many of the lesser issues, thus setting the stage for the ultimate test, which surely will come soon. In working with your attorneys and reviewing old cases, however, you should bear in mind that a favorable opinion by the CCPA in an early case may be useless in a modern application, as the Court has both reversed itself and been reversed on appeal. Consider, for example, the long-standing "mental steps" doctrine, which stated that anything that could be performed mentally was not subject matter for a patent.[13] Beginning in 1968 the CCPA scrapped this doctrine, stating instead that the ability to perform a process mentally should no longer foreclose patentability if the claims reveal that the process may also be performed *without* mental operations.[14]

As in the "mental steps" doctrine . . .

. . . Which may not be dead

But wait! In the Diehr case, which was decided by the Supreme Court in a very narrow 5–4 vote, the dissenting minority went to pains to point out that this doctrine had never been rejected by the high Court and that, in fact, subsequent Court decisions had implicitly utilized the approach. Thus there is little security in presuming that the "mental steps" doctrine (or its equivalent) is dead forever.

The majority of the Supreme Court would probably grant pure software a patent, but that majority is thin

The good news is that the majority of the Supreme Court has taken a consistent view in recent cases regarding the broad scope of patent protections, rejecting judicial precedent in favor of the legislative intent. Justice William Rehnquist, writing the majority opinion in the Diehr case, noted, "In cases of statutory construction, we begin with the language of the statute" and reiterated the Court's prior finding in *Perrin* v. *United States* (1979) that "courts 'should not read into the patent laws limitations and conditions which a legislature has not expressed.'" This is the long-term hope for software patentability, i.e., that the Supreme Court's narrow pro-patentability majority will no longer rely on old judicial tests and will look to the will of the legislature. If pure software *does* get the clear go ahead for patent protection from the Court, I suspect that it will be on this basis.

The Best Way to Proceed, if You Must

Your chances will be much improved if you can make an apparatus claim, versus a pure software claim

With uncertainty looming large, how should you proceed? While there is no safe way to file your claim, it *is* clear that a patent for an apparatus that includes software is far more likely to be issued and upheld than a patent for simply software. A 1969 case heard by the CCPA[15] held that "a machine programmed in a certain new and non-obvious way...is physically different from a machine without that program," leading to a spate of apparatus claims for software. Critics likened this to patenting "forward" and "reverse" in a gearbox, and the concept of physical transformation has been largely abandoned.

Another reason for avoiding this approach is to avoid any uncertainty that your apparatus patent will apply to the underlying software. Nonetheless, if your claim legitimately includes both hardware and software (or firmware) components, your chances are far greater that the courts will be favorably disposed, especially if it involves some inventive concept other than the software. If, for example, you have invented a software-driven apparatus for controlling the movement of a recording head on a disk drive, frame your claim on the basis of the invention's uniqueness and improvement in the prior art *as a whole.*

Avoid making claims related to new and improved methods of calculation or mathematical formulas, even if this is part of your apparatus (or program). While the Supreme Court did state (once again in the Diehr case) that patentability would apply "when a claim containing a mathematical formula implements or applies that formula in a structure or process which, when considered as a whole, is performing a function which the patent laws were designed to protect...," there is no advantage (or potential disadvantage) to making claims on other than the entire program, process, or apparatus and its novel nonalgorithmic elements.

Results count

Even if you make a pure software claim, remember to stress the product or result of the process in your claim. The courts must finally hurdle the issue of a process resulting in the subject matter being "transformed and reduced to a different state or thing." This definition was fine for a patent on nylon, but fails (as the Court has noted) for other than chemical processes. Nonetheless, your claim is seriously weakened if the *result* of your process is not of clear benefit.

Relate the claim to the process' use of the machine

The sorting of data is a good example. Even though the algorithm for performing the sort would probably fail the test of being a law of nature or mathematical formula (if not the "mental steps" doctrine), the sort should be eligible for a patent if it made new and unique use of the computer equipment in a nonobvious way to improve the state-of-the-art of sorting. In summary, the claim should be related to the process's (i.e., program's) unique and nonobvious use of the machine to produce a new or improved result.

Make the legal experts work for you, not vice versa

You are the businessman, and you should manage the patent process. Your attorney will be a rare duck indeed if he or she understands your invention and its application, novelty, etc., well enough to frame your claim for the maximum chance of success. You know enough now to make a decision to proceed to a patent application and to try to frame your claim for maximum chance of success, with a competent patent attorney's assistance. If you do not have a genuinely unique invention, or if your average competitor would find your invention obvious, or if you cannot identify where the laws of nature and mathematics end and your invention begins, save your money.

If you think your invention does meet these tests, the relevant history of court cases with a brief recital of the key points follows.

Relevant History

Before 1968 it was even *tougher*

Prior to 1968, software patents were regularly denied on the basis of the "mental steps" doctrine and the long-standing rule that ideas and scientific principles do not meet the statutory tests for patentability.[16] Similarly, patents that were sought for functions of a machine versus the machine itself were denied under the "function of the machine" doctrine. This 1853 doctrine[17] stated that you could not have a patent "...for the function or abstract effect of a machine, but only for the machine which produces it."

In 1966, a special panel, the President's Commission on the Patent System, alarmed by the potential burdens on the Patent Office, recommended that all software be denied patent protection.[18] As a result of these recommendations and prior judicial rulings, the Patent Office issued guidelines that declared a computer program unpatentable whether claimed as a process or as an apparatus.

The CCPA opened the doors in 1968

In 1968, however, just as these guidelines were adopted, the Court of Customs and Patent Appeals eliminated the long-standing "mental steps" and "function of a machine" guidelines. In rapid succession the CCPA found first that the "function of a machine" test was a judicial misinterpretation of Congress's will and of "the basic purpose of the patent system,"[19] and next that the ability to perform a process mentally would not by itself bar patentability.[20] Shortly thereafter, in one of its most dubious decisions, the CCPA held that a computer program physically transformed the computer into a different machine and thus software could be patentable as an apparatus.[21]

The "mental steps" test was declared dead

But the Supreme Court did not agree or dissent

Two more important CCPA decisions preceded the first Supreme Court test of the new guidelines. The first, in 1970,[22] reconfirmed that the "mental steps" doctrine was dead and substituted a new standard that permitted patentability for any process within the "technological arts." The second case[23] held that computers fell within this standard. Although this second case was reversed,[24] the Supreme Court did not challenge the lower court's new standards, but neither did it reaffirm the inapplicability of either the "mental steps" or "function of a machine" doctrines. Rather, the Court decided the issue on the narrow grounds that the application in question consisted of a mathematical procedure, an unpatentable process.

The Supreme Court simply reaffirmed the obvious, traditional tests are nearly an impossible hurdle for software

The CCPA's favorable view of software patent applications was not materially affected by this reversal. In the CCPA's view, the Supreme Court had merely held that software process claims for mathematical procedures were unacceptable, not that apparatus claims containing software were. Three CCPA cases refined this doctrine to state that apparatus and process claims for software were acceptable so long as the claim did not preempt a law of nature or mathematical formula.[25] The Supreme Court's refusal to grant Certiorari (i.e., to hear an appeal) in two of these cases for which it was requested did nothing to dampen the CCPA's belief that it was on the right track.

In 1978 the CCPA clarified its guidelines,[26] setting forth a two-step procedure for software-related claims. Such claims must first be examined to see if a mathematical formula is claimed, either directly or indirectly. If so, and only if so, the claim must then be examined to determine if it would seek to preempt that mathematical formula.

Some incentive concept, other than an improved method of calculation, is required

Almost coincidental to the CCPA's issuance of its new guidelines, however, the Supreme Court was clarifying its previous decision with another CCPA reversal.[27] The Court held that improved methods of calculation were not patentable, even if embodied in an apparatus. The Court said that any such mathematical formulas or methods of calculation should be treated as if they were a part of the prior art and the claim should be examined for "some other inventive concept." Further, the court ruled that a nonunique physical apparatus that served as a "back-end" for a mathematical process or method of computation would not make the claim statutory (i.e., patentable).[28]

Once again the CCPA was not dissuaded from its pro-software views, interpreting the Supreme Court's reversal more as a critique of the way a claim was drafted than of the underlying subject matter. The CCPA continued to support patents on claims for novel processes, even if the only new and unique element of the process was software.[29] In the previously referenced Diehr case and a companion case relating to "firmware,"[30] the Supreme Court seemed to agree, although its decisions were narrowly drawn to avoid the larger issues and decided by the narrowest of majorities. (The Diehr case was a 5–4 decision, while the companion Bradley case failed to reverse the CCPA on a 4–4 vote, the Chief Justice having disqualified himself.) The Court's rulings were solely on the basis of statutory subject matter (i.e., what can you patent), not on the validity of the claims. While the Court did reiterate that the presence of software, in and of itself, would not make a claim unstatutory, it did suggest that the claim might fail on the more conventional tests of obviousness, lack of novelty, and so on.

The CCPA persisted; patents should apply even if the only innovation is the software

. . . And the Supreme Court *seemed* to agree

. . . And Finally . . .

Beware the Court's articulate minority

This software patent history is instructive, but clear guidelines simply do not yet exist. The recent Diehr and Bradley cases suggest that a narrow majority of the Supreme Court is seeking a way to clarify when (not "if") software can be patentable subject matter. The Court's many previous appeals to the Congress to solve this problem legislatively are still pending, however, and the Court's minority holds a clearly articulated view that no software should be worthy of patent protection without such legislative sanction.

Bottom line: if you can, find an alternative

Before Congress acts, however, it is possible that some bold pioneer will not only invent a truly novel and nonobvious process that can be implemented solely as software, but will make the masochistic decision to press forward through almost certain rejection by the Patent Office and its Appeals Board, on to a probable victory at the CCPA, and finally to immortality as the decisive Supreme Court decision. Unless that person is you, I applaud you for reading this far, and I hope the balance of this book will offer you acceptable and less costly alternatives.

5 COPYRIGHT: THE (SOFTWARE) AUTHOR'S FRIEND

Introduction

This chapter will provide more detail on the single most important legal protection available to authors in general, and to software authors in particular. Unfortunately, especially for software authors, the rights conveyed by copyright are little understood or used. Even attorneys are frequently baffled by the application of old legal concepts to a new science.

What you need to know

What you need to know about copyright includes:

How to give "notice" and why this is critically important

What a copyright infringement is, and what remedies you have

The advantages, disadvantages, and mechanisms for registering a copyright

Why, when, and how to deposit your software with the Copyright Office

How to use copyright protection on the audio-visual portions of your software

The applicability of copyright to object code, "firmware," and databases

What constitutes "fair use" of your software

How copyright and trade secret protections fit together

Copyright protection overseas

The balance of this chapter will address each of these topics.

Much Abused and Underused

Your software already has a copyright around the world...it's automatic

An acquaintance once told me, "I don't use a copyright to protect my software." What he didn't understand was that, whether you want it or not, you have copyright protection by law. You don't need to fill out forms, register, or advise anyone of anything. Since 1978, copyright has been applied by federal statute to any work of authorship (which includes software) from the instant of creation. By treaty, these automatic protections extend around the world, once again with no overt action on your part. The protections provided are extremely powerful and, in certain cases, may be the *only* legal safeguards you have.

Copyright violations can subject the infringer to statutory damage awards of up to $50,000 per infringement, attorney's fees, and criminal penalties of $10,000 per infringement and up to one year in jail.

A victim of bad press and misunderstandings

Why, then, did my friend shy away from copyright? First, the changes in the copyright law have not been widely understood, and how copyright protection extends to all of the various forms software can take is still occasionally debated by less-informed attorneys and courts. Second, my friend confused the protections provided by law with registration of the copyrighted material. Registration in the United States provides some additional benefits to the copyright owner, but it is not required to have the copyright itself. Third, and probably most important, my friend assumed that you pick one form of protection or another—that copyright and trade secret protec-

tions, for example, are mutually exclusive. This is untrue, but widely
believed.

What Is a Copyright?

Copy control, not a monopoly on designs or ideas

A copyright is an author's legal right to control the reproduction and
distribution of his or her work for up to 100 years from its creation.
Copyright protection is granted by federal law and by international
treaty to all works of authorship that are "fixed in a tangible medium
of expression," including motion pictures, paintings and drawings,
choreographic works, sculptures, dramatic works, sound recordings,
and literary works (including software). Copyright protects the expression of someone's art; the sequence of sounds or sights, the creative way a story is told, the painter's presentation of color and form,
or the engineer's description of a process. What is *not* protected is
the creative idea that is embodied in the art or the process being
described.

Good news

The good news about copyright is indeed good; you receive
strong legal protections for your creations even if they are merely
new ways of expressing old things. Unlike a patent, copyright applies to works that are not unique and to algorithms. For the software developer this is ideal. As noted earlier, most software is the
clever implementation of an existing process or methodology. A
copyright will protect that implementation against copying, and
"copying" is broadly defined to include more than physical reproduction, as we will see.

. . . And bad

The bad news is that copyright does *not* protect
the underlying ideas and processes, nor does it preclude independent
inventions that might duplicate your work. These protections are
found in patent and trade secret laws, not copyright. Fortunately,
you can use all three.

The medium is not the message

Copyright also does not apply to the medium in which the work is
included, e.g., the silicon "chip" on which a "mask" is etched. In this
case, the mask is protected by copyright and reproducing the mask
would be a copyright infringement, but producing functionally similar chips would not be an infringement.

50, 75, or 100 years

Copyrighted works produced by individuals are protected for 50
years from publication. Corporate works are protected for 75 years
from publication or, if unpublished, for 100 years from creation.
Works produced by employees as a part of their regular duties, in the
absence of an agreement to the contrary, are considered to be the
employer's property. (See Chapter 7 for more on employer–employee
relations.)

Filing is easy

Copyright registration is procedurally simple: a $10 fee and a simple application form (class TX, the same one used for all literary works, available from the Copyright Office) are all that is necessary. Whether and what to deposit are more complex questions, which will be explored shortly.

Your Government Wants You (Protected)

The law has changed to meet new needs

Critics contend that the federal copyright laws have been bent and molded to include new forms of authorship, such as software. So what? Over the years the Act has been constantly revised to meet the Constitutional mandate to "...promote the Progress of Science and the Useful Arts, by securing for limited Times to Authors and Inventors the exclusive Right to their respective Writings and Discoveries." While the current Copyright Act is a poorly worded hodgepodge in need of rewrite, there is no question that Congress intended copyright to apply to *any* original work of authorship "fixed in a tangible medium of expression."

Rights of authors

The law grants the owner of a copyright "...the exclusive rights to do and to authorize any of the following: (1) to reproduce the copyrighted work..., (2) to produce derivative works..., (3) to distribute copies..., (4)...to perform the work publicly; and (5)...to display the copyrighted work publicly."[31]

Fix it and you're fixed

Since the Copyright Act of 1976, which went into effect January 1, 1978,[32] these rights apply automatically as you "fix" your work in any "tangible medium," i.e., write it on paper or store it on a disk. Works produced prior to 1978 had similar protections, but these were provided in part by the common laws of copyright, which were enforced on a state-by-state basis. Prior to 1978, only published and registered works enjoyed federal protection; state statutes and common laws protected unpublished works. As most software produced prior to 1978 is approaching old age or is already dead, I will concentrate on the current federal law.

Software is a literary work

Even if the plot is missing

Congress intended that all of the benefits of a copyright should apply to software, as the creation of software is a literary work of authorship, despite the unusual languages used by programmers. The Copyright Act defines "literary works" as "works expressed in words, numbers, or other verbal or numerical symbols or indicia, regardless of the material objects...in which they are embodied." In the legislative history that predated the 1976 copyright legislation, the House Report notes, "The term 'literary works' does not connote any criterion of literary merit...it includes...computer data bases and computer programs to the extent that they incorporate authorship in the programmer's expression of original ideas, as distinguished from the ideas themselves."[33] In 1980, in a technical revision to the 1976 law, Congress made the applicability of copyright to software even more explicit.[34]

Software in every form is protected, but only if it took some creative effort

Congress further intended that all of the various forms software can take should be protected. The CONTU report[35] predating the 1976 legislation, noted:

> The Commission has considered at length the various forms in which programs are fixed. Flowcharts, source codes and object codes are works of authorship in which copyright subsists, provided they are the product of sufficient intellectual labor to surpass the "insufficient intellectual labor" hurdle, which the instruction "apply hook to wall" fails to do.

Databases too

Copyright even extends to computer-based data if the database is an original work of authorship. While this topic is peripheral to the issue of software protection, a few key points are of relevance. A copyright applies even if the database (of software) is merely a rearrangement of facts that are already in the public domain.[36] Once again, it is the creative activity of arrangement and the resulting expression of the content, not the content itself, that is protected.

What This Means to You

"Copying" can cover a lot of territory

All five of the previously cited rights of authors have relevance to software. The most important may be the first two, as "reproduction" and "derivative works" cover a lot of territory. A novel, for example, is protected by copyright even when it is translated into a foreign language. The act of translation is either the creation of a copy or of a derivative work, depending on the presence of original authorship in the new copy. In both cases, copyright exists, even though the language changed in the process. It is the way something is expressed, not the precise language that carries the copyright. For example, even though neither the English "I'm fed up" nor the French equivalent, "J'en ai ras le bol," can be taken literally, the thought expressed is the same.

This is a key concept

As in writing a novel, creating a program can lead to infinite combinations of expression which, regardless of language, can be easily discerned. Once again, the legislative history of the current copyright law is instructive:

As under the present law, a copyrighted work would be infringed by reproducing it in whole or in any substantial part, and by duplicating it exactly by imitation or simulation. Wide departures or variations from the copyright works would still be an infringement as long as the author's "expression" rather than merely the author's "ideas" are taken.[37]

Which has been overlooked

The relevance of this to software has been lost on many attorneys, courts, and even to those in the industry. Fortunately, as Bob Dylan said, "The times they are a'changin.'"

Object code is a copy of the source code

Recent cases demonstrate real success by the producers of software in enforcing their rights to make copies. The courts are agreeing, for example, that object code is merely a copy of the original work, even though the language is different. The author could have written the novel in French (if he or she spoke the language) just as the programmer could have written in object code (if no easy means existed to translate from a simpler language). In neither case would the use of a different authoring language affect the copyright in the subsequent version, whether the translated work is considered to be a copy or a derivative work.

The source code may be a copy of the block diagram or decision table

This concept goes much further. If the original block diagram or decision table used by the programmer expressed the ideas or processes to be used in sufficient detail, the source code itself would be a copy of the block diagram (or, depending on whether additional work was required, a derivative work). The mechanized means that exist to convert decision tables into more conventional programming languages, for example, are merely making copies of the original work. As these "meta languages" evolve, the application of this concept will become more and more critical. Unless the original work contains "insufficient intellectual labor," the result of compiling or translating these new ultra-high-level languages will be copies of the original work, which are protected by copyright.

ROM, too

This follows all the way through the chain. The decision table, which is the original work, is copied into source code by a mechanical process. The source code is in turn copied into object code. The object code may be then copied into a different medium, e.g., read-only memory (ROM). The copyright on the decision table *should* protect the program in ROM. Courts have occasionally had trouble with this concept, but they are learning fast.

Other benefits, no drawbacks

There are other benefits to copyrights that this chapter will explore in detail. Briefly, however, they include worldwide recognition of identical or similar rights, statutory penalties for infringement, and ease of application. There are no drawbacks.

Copyright Rights Cut Two Ways

Copyright protections are statutory, i.e., the rights of authors and of users of copyrighted material are defined by law. Owners of copyrights frequently want more protection than those provided by the law and may, in fact, want to restrict the rights of the copyright recipient. This has led to industry practices in the distribution of software that range from questionable to laughable.

A contract requires two parties

As we will explore further in Chapter 8, a contract cannot be unilateral, i.e., you cannot make new demands on the buyer of a product or service after the sale. The conditions of sale must be agreed to by both parties in advance. Frequently, software vendors will include a "license agreement" with the products they sell at retail that purport to limit the rights of the buyer. Many of these "licenses" seek to limit the extent of the vendor's warranty, eliminate claims for consequential damages, and restrict product use. Even if a court were to find that these conditions constituted a valid contract between the parties, which is unlikely, most states have "consumer protection"

Sales to individuals follow different rules

laws that would override the waivers of obligations or liabilities in such agreements. While it is possible to waive "merchantablilty and fitness for a particular purpose" in transactions between commercial parties, these are legal obligations of a vendor that apply by legislation to most transactions with individuals. Furthermore, in a "sale" of a product it is unlikely that a court would uphold restrictive covenants on the buyer's subsequent rights (e.g., to resell or transfer the product). Any assumption by a vendor that legal obligations have been eliminated or that the buyer's use has been resricted by the mere inclusion of a "license agreement" with the product is pure folly.

Fair use is self-defining

With respect to copyright, there are certain "fair uses" of copyrighted materials as well as certain statutory rights of the purchaser that should be noted. "Fair use" of a copyrighted work is determined by the purpose of the use, the nature of the work, the percentage of the copyrighted work used, and the effect of such use on the commercial marketplace. The restrictions on use and transfer contained in many software "license agreements" are outside the reach of copyright and even those rights governed by copyright (e.g., the making

One test of unfair use is if a sale was lost

of copies and derivative works may be a "fair use" if these actions are not a substitute for a purchase). The making of backup copies is a specific right of the purchaser of software, for example. Even if the user could be shown to have "broken" a physical protection mechanism in order to make copies, a copyright violation would require that this copying was outside of the rights conveyed by law, and did not constitute a "fair use," regardless of the terms of an agreement.

Reasonable additions to the copyright protections can be had

The vendor of software through retail outlets has several options. The question of the "consideration" given in return for a user's waiver of rights is best handled through a transaction *subsequent* to purchase, e.g., the exchange of a service obligation by the vendor for an agreement by the buyer to limit his or her claims in the case of program error. This can be done with a simple postcard agreement that the buyer signs. With respect to copyright, it is best for the vendor to spell out the kinds of copies a user *can* make, always including those permitted by law (i.e., backup copies) as well as those that are forbidden (e.g., copies that would replace a sale). Remember, it is better to get the user to acknowledge reasonable obligations in exchange for specific benefits as this adds to your statutory copyright protection.

Notice: Your Most Important Obligation

Giving notice is required in the U.S.

Under the current copyright law a work must have a copyright notice if it "can be visually perceived directly or with the aid of a machine or device." "Visually perceptible copies" must have a notice "affixed to the copies in such a manner and location as to give reasonable notice of the claim of copyright."[38]

Failure can be costly

Failure to give notice or giving improper notice of your copyright can be a costly error. Although you can remedy an innocent failure to give proper notice within five years if only "a small number of copies" have been distributed and if ". . . a reasonable effort is made to add notice," doing it right from the outset is clearly preferable. Correcting your mistake also requires registration (which you might otherwise choose to avoid), and an innocent infringer is not penalized if notice was lacking at the time of the infringement.

It's easy to do

Giving notice is easy, but so is giving an improper notice. There is only one way a notice can be given to be sure that both domestic and international copyrights apply. Three elements are required: (1) the letter "c" in a circle, followed by (2) the name of the copyright owner, and (3) the date of first publication. For example:

© XYZ Corp. 1985

. . . And easy to do wrong

(C) does not work

This looks deceptively simple. The "c" in a circle is, for example, the *only* form of notice recognized worldwide, even though the U.S. recognizes the word *Copyright* and the abbreviation *Copr.* as alternatives. Ridiculous as it might seem, (c) is not equivalent to a "c" in a circle and does *not* constitute proper notice. As no standard character exists to represent the "c" in a circle, placement of notice can be difficult for machine-readable copies. The solution is to place a valid U.S. notice on the machine-readable portions and a valid worldwide notice on the printed labels and documents that accompany the machine-readable material. For example:

© COPYRIGHT XYZ Corp. 1985 ALL RIGHTS RESERVED.

Spelling counts

where the circle around the "c" is closed on all external labels. Although a meaningless addition in the United States, the "(c)" may help elsewhere, as so far only the U.S. has ruled the "(c)" does not meet the international standard. Note further that "Copyrighted," "Copyr.," or any other string of characters than the two prescribed by law will be treated as if no notice had been given.

...And the date must be correct

You can "publish" by lending

Failure to supply the proper (or any) date can also invalidate your notice. The date provided must be no later than one year from the date of first "publication." For copyright purposes, "publication" is a defined term that does not have the commercial meaning. In the context of the copyright laws, "publication" means "distribution of copies . . . by sale or other transfer of ownership or by rental, lease, or lending."

...So notice on every-thing is a good idea

This broad definition and the lack of any potential harm from an early notice suggests that the date of creation should be used. For corporate developers the protections provided by copyright extend at least seventy-five years from this date, far beyond the anticipated life of any software product.

Giving notice doesn't affect a claim of trade secrecy

As we will review in more detail in Chapter 6, the claim of a "publication" date and the provision of notice has no affect on other relevant protections (e.g., the state trade secret laws). Even the Copyright Office's regulations note that " . . . affixation of a copyright notice on unpublished works may not necessarily evidence publication."[39] A series of court decisions has reaffirmed this principle. In one key decision,[40] the court stated, "The court is not willing to concede that, as a matter of law, the mere act of affixing a copyright notice . . . voids any claim of secrecy . . . ."

Update the notice with the software

And keep copies

As your software is updated you should expand the notice to include the multiple years that apply to the old and new portions. Never simply change the notice to the most recent year, as the notice would fail to meet the one-year test for most of the work and it could be claimed that you were seeking to extend the term of protection. Keep copies of each version of the software to demonstrate the original and subsequent claims.

The Copyright Office has published guidelines for the affixation of notice.[41] For machine-readable works, the guidelines say:

**Current Copyright
Office guidelines
are flexible**

g. *Works reproduced in machine-readable copies*
  . . . each of the following constitute examples of acceptable methods
  of affixation and position of notice:
  (1) . . . on visually perceptible printouts it appears . . . near the title,
  or at the end . . . ;
  (2) . . . is displayed at the user's terminal at sign on;
  (3) . . . is continously on terminal display; or
  (4) A legible notice . . . on a gummed or other label securely affixed to
  the copies or . . . container used as a permanent recepticle for the
  copies.

**Combine your notices
and put them
everywhere**

Note, however, that these are not to be considered complete. You
can put notices anywhere. Also, you cannot have too many notices; it
is better to err on the high side. If your software is a trade secret or is
covered by license agreement you can and should combine the various notices into one clear statement. For example:

```
************************** NOTICE **************************
       PROPRIETARY AND CONFIDENTIAL MATERIAL.
     DISTRIBUTION, USE, AND DISCLOSURE RESTRICTED
         BY LICENSE. (c) COPYRIGHT XYZ Corp. 1985
                 ALL RIGHTS RESERVED

*************************************************************
```

There is more you should know about trade secret notice, but
that will be found in the next chapter. First, let's review the other
advantages of copyright, starting with the reasons to register your
software.

The Benefits and Drawbacks of Registration

Object code is exempt

In theory, every work must be deposited with the Library of Congress within three months of its "publication," whether or not it is
ever registered with the Copyright Office. In practice, however, there
are no penalties for failure to deposit a work unless the Copyright Office makes a specific demand that you do, and this has never been
their practice. In addition, all machine-readable works are exempt
from this mandatory deposit requirement,[42] which means that unless
your source programs are "published," deposit is required only if and
when you choose to register.

**As are works you
don't "publish"**

While "publication" for copyright purposes can mean the licensing of even a single copy, this will usually *not* apply to your flowcharts and other design documents, and possibly not even to your
source code. As unpublished works, these are also exempt from any

statutory deposit requirements. Accordingly, the usual practices followed in software distribution lend themselves to copyright protection, with no obligation to register or deposit even "published" object code.

So, if you don't have to, why register?

Your copyright exists whether or not you register and deposit your work. There are enforcement advantages, however, to registering your work with the Copyright Office and depositing representative copies. You cannot bring a suit until you register, although you can register your work just before you go to court. More important, infringements that took place prior to your registration are not subject to statutory penalties which, among other things, include your potential recovery of legal fees and up to $50,000 in statutory damages.[43]

But you *could* lose more than you gain if you choose to deposit source code

If registration takes place after an infringement, you can still seek to have criminal penalties applied to the infringer, including up to $10,000 in fines and one year in jail. You can seek an injunction to prevent further distribution of unauthorized copies, regardless of whether you registered before the infringement, and you can still ask a civil court to award you actual damages or lost profits. The availability of these protections without the need to register and concerns about the effect of source code deposit on trade secret protections have persuaded many companies to defer registration until an actual infringement action is to be pursued.

Can you have it both ways: register without disclosure?

Determining lost profits is extremely difficult, however, which makes the statutory award of up to $50,000 per infringement very attractive. Also, attorneys' fees can be substantial in a copyright infringement suit. But, can you register and not disclose invaluable trade secrets?

Yes, exceptions to the deposit rules are possible

By law, copyright deposits must be open to public examination. Also by law, however, the Register of Copyrights can exempt certain classes of materials from the deposit regulations or provide alternative forms of deposit.[44] In the case of printed examinations, for example, the Register permits a diagonal strip from the test to be deposited, an insufficient amount of material to allow a test-taker to discern the questions and their answers, but enough material to identify the work. The Register can also provide special relief on a case-by-case basis anytime deposit would involve the disclosure of secret materials.

. . . And the rules are changing

The current Copyright Office regulations for software are deficient in not providing an automatic mechanism for the protection of trade secrets. The Copyright Office recognizes this and is in the middle of a reexamination of its deposit requirements for software. Even the current regulations, however, permit you to work your way around the problem of disclosure.

Today, they want some of your source code, . . . not object code

The Copyright Act requires that the "best edition" of your work be deposited for registration purposes. The Copyright Office's current interpretation of this is, in the case of software, to require the deposit of the source code. What they want today are two copies of an "identifying portion" of the program, stated to be the first and last twenty-five pages of a source listing. They claim that they need this to determine that the program is indeed "an original work of authorship." The Copyright Office feels that it cannot make such a determination from the object code, a puzzling complaint as they will register works written in the most remote foreign languages, presumably without the benefit of such a determination.

. . . But they will take it under protest

If you insist, the Copyright Office will accept object code in lieu of source code, but only under their so-called "Rule of Doubt." This requires that you tell the office in writing that the work is indeed an original work of authorship. Many companies have chosen this tactic, presuming that the relative obscurity of object code to human readers protects their trade secrets and that the slightly clouded copyright certificate is not of great significance. I disagree, especially with the first premise.

Deposit of any secret is a big problem, however

If you claim that your object code contains trade secrets, there is no reason to expect that a court would not find deposit (which, remember, includes mandatory disclosure) as evidence of a waiver of trade secret protections, whether or not anyone ever tried to get at them.

Which you can avoid

Until the regulations change, there is no reason not to live with the ones now in existence. You must do a little extra work to insure that you don't compromise trade secrets, but it is clearly worth it.

Do you really have a secret?

First, determine if you really have trade secret rights to protect (see Chapter 6). You may discover that you have already disclosed the "secrets" of your software, in which case copyright protection is all you have, and complete registration and deposit is to your benefit.

If so, ask for relief

In return for a viable alternative

If you do have confidential information to protect, first send a letter to the Copyright Office requesting special relief[45] under 37 CFR sections 202.19(e) and 202.20(d). State specifically the nature of the trade secret you cannot disclose. The few such requests made to date have been denied, but, as previously noted, this issue is in flux.[46] Offer to disclose your software to the office on a confidential basis and, if they wish, to leave a "representative sample" of the work for deposit purposes that would not compromise the secret.

Exemption chances increase with disclosure

The Copyright Office notes that it "prefers to receive a deposit disclosing as much authorship as possible, without divulging trade secrets. . . . Generally the more generous the authorship disclosure, the more likely the request for special relief will be granted."[47] If there is no way to disclose what the Copyright Office would prefer to have (i.e., " 'batches' of authorship that would be the equivalent of 'sentences' or 'paragraphs' "[48]), offer to submit a segment of your work that would not disclose confidential material but that would be sufficient to identify the work in an infringement suit (e.g., a listing of the middle ten characters from each line of source code).

You can work with the current rules, if you have to

If your request is denied, organize your source program so that the first twenty-five and the last twenty-five pages do not contain trade secrets. Although cumbersome, I take the position that this is the current mechanism provided to you by the Copyright Office so they can insure that your work is indeed copyrightable material and so you can preserve the confidentiality of key portions. It helps that, for most large programs written in high-level languages, data definitions, file layouts, and storage allocations normally occur at the beginning and cross-reference lists and label addresses occur at the end. Even if this is not the case, or if the program is naturally less than fifty 8 1/2″ × 11″ pages long, you can and should pad it by including more commentary and nonconfidential documentation.

. . . And gain some advantage on the way . . .

As deposited material is useful in any infringement action, I recommend that you deposit some encryptified portion of the middle portion of your program as well (e.g., a few characters from each line of code). Precede the encryptified portion with a note that the material that follows has been only partially deposited to preserve the underlying trade secrets in the material.

Object Code and ROM

The law *seems* clear

The copyright law states that "copyright protection subsists . . . in original works of authorship fixed in *any tangible medium of expression,* now known or later developed, *from which they can be perceived, reproduced, or otherwise communicated,* either directly or *with the aid of a machine* or device" (emphasis mine). This language seems straightforward. It suggests that all of a program's forms should be protected, whether easily perceived by humans or not. It does not suggest that a copyright on the underlying software would in any way grant controlling rights over the medium in which it is fixed (e.g., the silicon chip). Neither is a distinction made between software used to control the machine and software that performs an application.

. . . But it was challenged

Unfortunately, in several early tests of the new copyright law the defense raised all of these questions, claiming that object code, especially "operating system" software, was not sufficiently "fixed in a tangible medium" and that a copyright on software in read-only memory (ROM) would grant control over a "utilitarian object," i.e., the silicon chips in which the ROM resided.

Reason is winning

The courts now say that both object code and ROM are subject to copyright

Fortunately, these arguments only served as temporary barriers to reason. Recent court decisions have made it more and more clear that copyright protections apply regardless of the form of the program or the media on which it resides. One court noted that you must always make ". . .the distinction between the work which is the subject of copyright and the tangible medium in which the work is fixed."[49] Another stated categorically that "a silicon chip is a tangible medium of expression."[50] Yet another noted, "We cannot accept the defendant's suggestion that would afford an unlimited loophole by which infringement of a computer program is limited to copying the computer program text but not to duplication of the computer program fixed on a silicon chip," and that use of a utilitarian object to store the program (i.e., ROM) no more restricted use of that object than "an author with a valid copyright restricts the use of books."[51] Object codes, whether used to operate the computer or perform an application, have recently been held copyrightable in a series of cases.[52]

While your attorney will caution you that nothing is certain, it would seem your chances for successfully defending your software copyright, regardless of form, are increasing daily. If your program includes a series of re-creatable visual displays and sounds you can also register it as an audio-visual work. This is especially useful for games and educational programs, but should be considered for most software.

Registering the Audio-Visual Portions of Your Program

What is an audio-visual work?

The Copyright Act defines audio-visual works as "works that consist of a series of related images which are intrinsically intended to be shown by the use of machines or devices such as projectors, viewers, or electronic equipment, together with accompanying sounds, if any, regardless of the nature of the material objects, such as films or tapes, in which the works are embodied."

The images and sounds produced by your software qualify

This definition clearly includes images and sounds that are embodied in software. Some have claimed that the production of images by a computer is not "an original work of authorship," but a court recently reviewed this question and held[53] that "an author's work does not become any less original after he has found a means to replicate it." The reviewing appellate court held that "the repetitive sequence of a substantial portion of the sights and sounds of the game qualifies for copyright protection as an audiovisual work."

The courts have not yet agreed, however, on how copyright protection will apply to interactive programs, i.e., where the user of the software contributes to the flow. The issue is clear for software that produces a specific series of images and/or sounds; the analogy to motion picture film and other means of recording audio-visual works is exact. But what if the software can follow a nearly infinite number of paths depending on the actions of the user? In this case it has been claimed that the user is "co-authoring" a new work that is, at best, a derivative of the original.

The counter-argument is that the richness of possible image sequences has nothing whatsoever to do with the issue of copyright protection. It would be theoretically possible to produce every conceivable sequence and as each would be subject to copyright, so should the whole. How does this differ from an encyclopedia, for example, which is never read in sequence? Access to the work is controlled by the user. Even if the "work" resulting from the interaction with the user is a derivative of the original, isn't the right to produce derivative works one of the author's privileges? These are questions that must be answered. For now, however, there are certain clear rules that do apply.

Your software can be registered as an audio-visual work by depositing videotapes (for example) of the sequence of sights and sounds produced. Clearly, for video games with an "attract mode" or for interactive data entry routines that present a fixed series of images to the user, those images and sounds should be included in the deposit. If the software runs in an interactive "play" or "execute" mode, include as many sequences as possible on the videotape. While this is of uncertain value, courts *have* found copyright infringement in analogous cases where the exact sequence of sights and sounds differed from the original, e.g., in sound recordings where the underlying theme is so similar as to be deemed an infringement.

Remember, however, the copyright protection you seek extends only to your method of expressing yourself, not to the underlying ideas. Another game with a similar set of characters and play objectives or another interactive tax preparation package will not infringe your copyright simply because you had the first such product on the market.

The specific procedures to be followed are simple, despite the Copyright Office's slowness in modifying its regulations, forms, and procedures to accommodate program submittals. To register a program with audio-visual components, two separate forms must be

Do you become a co-author when you play a video game or interact with the software?

Some issues await court decisions

Deposit a video tape of the visual portions

To protect your creative expression

. . . Versus your ideas

Actual filing is simple

supplied to the Copyright Office: Form TX to register the program and Form PA to register the audio-visual work embodied in the program. Each must be accompanied by a $10 filing fee and representations of the copyright notices as they appear on the works. The Copyright Office notes that for audio-visual registrations " 'special relief' from the deposit requirement must be requested because there are no special provisions in the Copyright Office regulations for such works." Detailed instructions are provided with the forms themselves and in the related Copyright Office publications, particularly ML-212. These forms and publications can be ordered by mail or phone (see reference 4).

Foreign Protections

U.S. copyright provides worldwide protections

U.S. copyrights are respected throughout most of the industrialized world; this is one of the great advantages of copyright. Most countries, by treaty,[54] recognize another country's copyrights, without any action on the part of the copyright holder. While the United States tends to lead the rest of the world in the application of copyright protection to software, a body of foreign case law is building, which suggests that similar treatment can be expected abroad.

In Japan, for example, the Copyright Council debated the key points and concluded that software was protected and that object code was merely a copy of the source code, noting that "even though there is some change, or reproduction or expansion in the work, to the extent that the identity of the work is unchanged, the result is a reproduction of the work and it is covered by the right to reproduce."

But serious problems remain

Protectionism and bad decisions will continue

The application of copyright to software outside of the United States is in a state of flux, however, and it will be several years before the apparent strength of a U.S. copyright in foreign markets will be completely established. Despite the enlightened position of Japan's Copyright Council, as noted above, Japan's Ministry of International Trade and Industry (MITI) recently proposed that software be removed from copyright protection and treated as industrial property under patent law. On another front, a federal judge in Australia recently ruled that software could not be protected by copyright because "it was not deemed to be a literary work within the meaning of the Copyright Act." This decision was subsequently overturned.

... But the weight of law and the forces of the market favor copyrights

Most observers do not expect protectionist moves like MITI's or uninformed judicial opinions to disrupt the international trend toward a unified stance on copyright protection for software. It is true that the international treaties now in existence, most notably the Universal Copyright Convention of 1952, *do* leave room for interpretation, but the actions cited above are exceptions to a general trend that supports the current U.S. position. Moreover, the weight of economic pressure in this area is extraordinary. In the Australian case, for example, steps were taken by the government to modify the law just days after the first judge's decision and before an appeal had been filed, primarily as a result of threats by foreign corporations to cease doing business in Australia. Despite the uncertainties, copyright remains the most viable (and perhaps the only) protection mechanism available outside of the United States. This is clearly an area where specially trained legal counsel is a *must*.

As in the United States, proving a copyright infringement in a foreign jurisdiction involves demonstrating such things as striking similarity between the works, that creation of the infringing work took an unreasonably short period of time, and that the infringer had access to the infringed work.

Beware of "moral rights"

Many country's copyright laws grant "moral rights" to the author. Essentially, these rights allow the author to protect his or her reputation, i.e., to prevent changes in the work that could be damaging to his or her reputation. As in the United States, works created by employees (if part of their normal responsibilities) belong to the employer and the "moral rights" issue does not apply. Works done by outside contractors are a different matter, however, in that any revisions or additions to the work could require a waiver from the author. This is generally not a problem, but you should check with your local attorney if you are purchasing software from third parties in foreign territories.

You can cut off foreign knock-offs by an appeal to the ITC

One last note on foreign protections: The International Trade Commission has jurisdiction over imports from foreign territories. The ITC can restrict imports that infringe on a U.S. copyright and has already done so,[25] demonstrating a fairly competent knowledge of software-related issues in the process. An appeal to the ITC could be a quick way to end foreign imports of copies of your software, but preventing distribution abroad will have to be left to the foreign courts.

The customs service can seize counterfeit goods

To take advantage of the ITC's jurisdiction over imports and the Custom Service's ability to seize counterfeit products, a special registration of your copyrights and brand names with the Customs Service in Washington is required. Once registered, the Customs Service can seize incoming counterfeits and then refer the case to federal prosecutors for prosecution. While the most common use of this procedure to date has been to prevent the import of counterfeit computer hardware and operating systems (both Apple and IBM have registered and requested the special protections available), there is no reason that pure software, absent the hardware, would not qualify.

6 TRADE SECRETS

Introduction

Neither a patent nor a copyright protects "know-how"

In Chapter 4 we learned that, subject to court approval, a patent could give us a monopoly on our invention if it was truly unique, new, and nonobvious; we also learned that this would be highly unlikely for software. Even if a patent could be obtained, however, patents do not extend to the valuable business "know-how," which is frequently the secret of an enterprise's success. Chapter 5 explained that a copyright will give us strong protections against unauthorized copying but, powerful as that is, underlying designs, ideas, processes, and (once again) "know-how" are not protected. In this chapter we will learn how the concept of trade secrecy can fill this void.

Trade secret laws can vary from state to state

Unlike patents and copyrights, which are granted by federal law, trade secret protections derive from common law concepts enforced by the states. Accordingly, this form of protection could vary from locale to locale, although in practice there is a high degree of consis-

**. . . But the principles
of trade secrecy
are consistent**

tency across state lines, as local courts tend to look to relevant cases from other jurisdictions in reaching conclusions. Furthermore, a majority of the states have codified at least a part of their trade secret and/or unfair competition law. An examination of the differences between state laws is beyond the scope of this text, unless the variation is a noteworthy exception or represents a legislative trend. In general, however, the principles involved are amazingly consistent.

**Even outside of the
U.S.A. (but less so)**

This is far less true outside of the United States. Trade secret protections *do* exist elsewhere; in fact, the United States is one of only a handful of industrialized nations without a federal trade secret law. Japan's 1907 penal code, for example, makes disclosure of a trade secret a criminal offense. Nonetheless, there is no international consistency or treaty governing trade secrets or the related issue of unfair competition. These concepts are at the very root of the free enterprise system, however, and the application of good business practice to the protection of trade secrets cannot damage any claim you might have to make in a foreign court, but be sure to retain competent local counsel. As trade secrets are defined locally and interpreted by local courts, the focus of this book will be on generally applicable principles and on their U.S. application.

**A trade secret is easily
lost, relatively ineffec-
tive against unrelated
third parties, and not
appropriate for
mass marketing**

Because of the limited nature of trade secret protection it should *never* be the only form of protection employed. A trade secret is easy to lose; any disclosure of the secret, regardless of circumstance, will forever eliminate a claim of trade secrecy. Furthermore, trade secret protections, unlike patent or copyright protections, are generally ineffective against unrelated third parties (e.g., the customer of the ex-employee who appropriated your trade secret). For mass-merchandized software, trade secrecy is largely inappropriate, at least as it relates to the distributed product. Despite these drawbacks, trade secrecy combined with copyright and, where possible, strong contractual protections can be a powerful combination. Accordingly, every business should have an active trade secrets program, however limited.

**Any valuable business
information can be a
trade secret, including
the design
techniques in
your software**

As we will see in greater detail shortly, anything that has value to a business and is kept secret is a trade secret. Clearly, software can meet this test. Thus, unlike a patent, which can only apply to machines, manufactured goods, matter, and processes, a trade secret can apply to any and all of a business's valuable information. Unlike a copyright, which prevents unauthorized copying, trade secret protection extends beyond "the form of expression" to the secret itself. The most famous trade secret, for example, is probably a relatively simple process: how to make Coca-Cola. While copying the piece of paper on which this formula is written would be a copyright violation, learning the process in any unfair or unauthorized way (other than reinventing it) would be a trade secret violation.

There are legitimate competing claims on most trade secrets

Trade secret protections are powerful because they are so broad, but due to their generality they are difficult to get, keep, and defend. Because there are legitimate competing claims to the same business information—claims by employees, customers, the employer, agents, and competitors—the settlement of trade secret cases is a difficult balancing job for the courts. If the enterprise has failed to rigorously protect this information, it can and frequently will lose its claim to one of these other interested parties.

The most common trade secret claims involve ex-employees

Most trade secret claims arise out of the departure of key employees to a competitive venture. The sensitive information frequently concerns marketing as well as technical matters. In fact, the most common trade secret claim involves the misappropriation of customer and prospect lists. The most frequent defense is that the information was either never a secret or that, through sloppy practices, it is no longer a secret. In almost every case, however, it is clear that a better understanding of what was secret and who owned it, coupled with good business practices, could have avoided costly litigation.

A successful trade secrets program must be an integral part of day-to-day operations

Prevention of conflict is critical

Good business practice as it relates to trade secrecy almost always involves a formal, rigorous program encompassing everything from contractual relationships to employee relations. Trade secrecy programs cannot be superimposed on a business; they must be a natural part of everyday life. Simply stamping everything "CONFIDENTIAL," for example, serves no purpose and may even help *defeat* a legitimate trade secrecy claim. Conversely, something as simple and natural as a well-written employee handbook, setting out the obligations and rights of the employer and employee, can be a *very* effective tool, not only in pursuing a trade secrecy claim but in avoiding the conflict in the first place. After introducing some important definitional issues, the information in this chapter will help you establish a preventive program to avoid trade secret litigation altogether and give you a better chance of success if such litigation ever proves necessary.

What Is a Trade Secret?

Trade secret = valuable secret + use for competitive advantage

There is no single definition of a trade secret. In general, however, a trade secret is any business secret that provides a competitive advantage. Unlike a patent, a trade secret need not be novel. As with material subject to copyright, a trade secret can involve a compilation of publicly available information; a customer list is a good exam-

. . . E.g., customer lists

ple. It is the commercial value of the list and its confidential use that establishes its trade secrecy, not the actual contents. Independent creation of the list by a third party would be perfectly acceptable, however. It is only when valuable business property (i.e., the secret) is misappropriated and used to gain an unfair competitive advantage that trade secret rights apply.

Despite the informality of trade secrecy, a majority of states use one formal definition, which was set out in 1939. A trade secret is

Most states use one definition

With six tests for trade secrecy

any formula, pattern, device, or compilation of information which is used in one's business . . . to obtain an advantage over competitors who do not know or use it. The subject matter of a trade secret must be secret . . . so that except by the use of improper means there would be difficulty in acquiring the information. An exact definition of a trade secret is not possible. Some factors to be considered in determining whether given information is one's trade secret are: (1) the extent to which it is known outside of his business; (2) the extent to which it is known by employees and others involved in his business; (3) the extent of measures taken by him to guard the secrecy of the information; (4) the value of the information to him and his competitors; (5) the amount of effort or money expended by him in developing the information; (6) the ease or difficulty with which the information could be properly acquired or duplicated by others.[56]

Software can be a trade secret if it has unique logic, coherence, and commercial feasibility

The "information" referred to in this definition can include data, facts, experience, knowledge, and "know-how." As one key court case decided, software is included if it has "unique logic and coherence" and "commercial feasibility."[57] However, the subject matter in a claimed trade secret cannot be "public knowledge or of a general knowledge in the trade or business."[58] For example, while the Coca-Cola formula is a trade secret, general information about the soft-drink business is not. This concept of general business knowledge will be of critical importance when we review the rights of employees to your/their inventions.

A Contractual Relationship Must Exist

A secret is only a secret if everyone who knows it agrees

A trade secret cannot be disclosed to anyone and still be a secret unless there is agreement between the parties to protect it. There can be *implicit* agreements, of course, that arise in the course of well-understood business dealings, such as those between an employer and an employee, but the agreement must nonetheless exist. While general

Implicit agreements *can* exist, but written agreements are *always better*

Some business information just isn't a trade secret . . .

Including general industry knowledge and, in certain instances, employee inventions

Even if you pay an employee to develop trade secrets, you may not have an exclusive right to the results unless you have a specific agreement

Third parties are not normally bound to protect your secrets

Trade secrecy + copyright = success

publication of a secret will destroy its trade secrecy forever,[59] disclosure under implied covenants of secrecy will not.[60]

In the absence of a written agreement it is unlikely that information disclosed without a notice of confidentiality will be considered a trade secret unless it can be clearly shown that the recipient would have had reason to expect, either from the way it was disclosed or based on knowledge of the competitive advantage it provided, that the disclosure was made with an understanding of confidentiality.[61] When an employer provides training, for example, that is similar to what the employee would have received in a competitive position, the disclosure will generally *not* be in a context that would allow the employer to prevent use of the knowledge by the employee in a subsequent position.

As most trade secrecy claims involve ex-employees, we will examine the entire subject of employee relations in the following chapter. In general, however, trade secrecy does not extend to the knowledge an employee gains about a particular type of business, general industry knowledge, knowledge that an employee would have obtained in a competitive position, and, in certain cases, knowledge developed by the employee at work.

Employee inventions are a most difficult area. Chapter 7 will explore this topic in greater depth, but for now a good general rule can be stated. Employee developments that do not incorporate other trade secrets disclosed by the employer and that were developed without significant employer contributions of supervision, facilities and materials, extraordinary expense, etc., will, *in the absence of a written agreement to the contrary,* belong to the employee. The employer will have a "shop right" to use the trade secret but could not prevent the employee's use of the information in subsequent employment, even if the employment is with a competitor. The message to all employers should be clear: Written agreements are essential for employees who are expected to develop trade secrets *and* any disclosure of trade secrets, provision of materials (e.g., computer access), or other contributions to the development of a trade secret should be carefully documented.

A significant drawback to trade secret protections arises directly from the need for the parties to agree to maintain confidentiality, even at the level of third parties who might access the secret (e.g., the employees of your customer). While a strong contractual relationship may exist between you and your customer, there is usually no way to establish a contractual relationship with the customer's employees and agents. Unlike a copyright infringement in which you could enjoin reproduction of the copyrighted work, enjoining a third-party accessor of a trade secret from using the secret can be difficult or impossible. This is another reason why a marriage of trade secret and copyright protections is desirable wherever possible.

What You Must Do

Independent invention and reverse engineering are not trade secret violations

Therefore, the physical protection of a secret is essential

As a rule, the more sensitive the information in a trade secret, the more extensive must be the measures used to protect it. For software, this can mean a combination of physical and procedural methods. Programs distributed through retail stores, for example, are generally object programs. Trade secrecy provides no barrier to someone "reverse engineering" from the object program by first "disassembling" it and then rewriting it using the disassembled program as a guide. While this may be a copyright violation (if a copy or derivative work results), it is not a trade secret violation, regardless of the extent of the protections afforded the source programs and other materials used to create the commercial product. For this reason, trade secrecy would apply to software sold at retail only if physical barriers (e.g., encryption) were used to prevent disclosure.

Any trade secret requires extensive active protection to remain a secret. The following is a partial list of the types of protections that should be used with software:

Restrict access, write procedures

1. Access to the source programs, flowcharts, design documents, etc., should be restricted to employees, agents, and contractors with a "need to know." There should be written procedures governing access and physical security to protect against casual disclosure. For example, trade secret materials should never be left in open work areas or generally available to any employee with a terminal. Good practice will by and large include physical security over any work areas where trade secrets are generally available and a "lock-up" program for these documents when they are not in use.

Mark all confidential materials

Itemize classes of confidential materials

2. Materials containing trade secrets should always carry a notice to that effect. Since "confidential" is a broader definition than "trade secret" (confidential information does not have to provide a competitive advantage or be in current use), marking documents "confidential" is the preferred approach. The notice should appear prominently, preferably on every page or on every

other page in a fan-folded listing. Written procedures should exist, defining what information is confidential; the list should be as precise as possible. The use of "confidential" warnings should be constrained to items on the list.

**Get employee
agreement
before hiring**

Renew annually

Education is key

3. Written procedures should exist to govern an employee's rights to access and use trade secrets, preferably as part of the "employee handbook" issued to all employees *prior* to their employment. Employees should formally agree to these rights and procedures at hiring and at least annually thereafter. Agreement should include the assignment of all inventions and discoveries made on company time and/or with company assistance to the company. Institute a formal program to educate employees on their responsibilities in trade secret protection.

Identify breaches

4. A formal program should exist to identify breaches of security. For example, sales and service personnel should have a specific duty to report any misuse of company information by agents, prospects, or customers.

**Put notices every-
where; include the
copyright notice**

5. Programs distributed as trade secrets should contain external as well as internal notice that the material is confidential, copyrighted, and (if applicable) subject to contractual restrictions on distribution and use. As noted in Chapter 5, a comprehensive notice would be:

*************************** NOTICE ***************************
PROPRIETARY AND CONFIDENTIAL MATERIAL. DIS-
TRIBUTION, USE, AND DISCLOSURE RESTRICTED BY
LICENSE. (c) Copyright XYZ Corp. 1985
ALL RIGHTS RESERVED.

****

The circle around the "c" should be closed on all printed materials and external labels.

**Get signed
nondisclosure
agreements *before*
you disclose**

6. No disclosure of the trade secret or distribution of trade secret materials should be made without a written nondisclosure agreement. This is the most difficult area to enforce because sales frequently hang on disclosure and it is not unusual for software to be installed before a formal contract is signed. Nonetheless, while an understanding of confidentiality can apply in anticipation of a formal agreement, general distribution without formal agreement would almost certainly defeat a claim of trade secrecy.

Log all distributions

All nondisclosure agreements should be retained and a log of distributions of materials should be kept. Ideally, every software

**Number each
software package**

**Never "sell"
licensed software**

**Pass the obligation to
protect to agents
and employees**

**Incorporate some
easily identified but
meaningless instruc-
tions or names**

**Get "work for hire"
agreements with all
outside contractors**

Recapture information

**Destroy or control
all scrap**

package should contain a unique number (externally and in the software) that should be logged against the nondisclosure or license agreement.

Software distributed under license agreements should never be "sold," as legislative and judiciary restrictions can apply to the passage of restrictive covenants. Customer agreements should specify that trade secrets are being passed by license and should bind the recipient to acquire appropriate guarantees of secrecy from agents and employees. The agreement should also explicitly allow for injunctive relief in the case of a breach.

7. It is an excellent practice to include a few "nonsense" instructions in your software (i.e., instructions that function, but to no useful advantage). Adding A to B then subsequently subtracting A from B, for example, would serve no purpose. If the software is misappropriated, however, evidence that this was deliberately incorporated to identify infringement would provide a valuable "smoking gun." This same technique works with other materials as well. For instance, customer and prospect lists can be seeded with phoney names in order to demonstrate misappropriation. Obviously, the use of such a technique can neither be widely known by your employees nor obvious to an outsider.

8. *Always* have a written agreement with outside contractors specifying that (1) any software or documentation developed by the contractor is a "work made for hire" as that term is defined in Section 101 of the Copyright Act, (2) the contractor will protect any trade secrets supplied or developed under contract, and (3) any and all patent, copyright, or other property rights developed by the contractor are the sole and exclusive property of the hiring party. Lack of a contract in work-for-hire instances can be a serious oversight.[62]

9. Always recapture any confidential information provided to clients, agents, prospects, or employees at the end of their "need to know." In the case of customers and agents it is good practice to require the return or destruction of all materials marked "confidential" upon the expiry of their contract.

10. Have a secure method for destroying or discarding material containing trade secrets. Computer listings are the most difficult of such materials to control. Nonetheless, permitting employees to take source program listings home, for example, without safeguards on their protection, return, and ultimate disposal could help defeat a subsequent trade secrecy claim.

Conduct regular audits

11. Conduct regular audits of your trade secrecy (and copyright) programs. Document audits as proof of your seriousness should litigation ever be required.

Termination procedures should recapture secrets and include a reminder of continuing obligations

12. Establish a formal termination procedure to insure that all confidential materials have been returned by departing employees, including any notebooks or other documents the employee may have created that contain protected information. Give the terminating employee a verbal and written reminder of the terms of confidentiality (and, if applicable, noncompete) agreements that will survive the termination. If appropriate, notify the new employer in writing of these obligations. Be careful, however, not to unfairly restrict an employee's subsequent job opportunities or use an employment agreement as a means of harassment. This whole topic is important enough to warrant a separate chapter, which follows immediately.

Marrying Trade Secrets, Patents, and Copyrights

Federal law always prevails

"Equivalent rights" are preempted

A state cannot override a federal law. This creates tensions when there are similar rights being protected on a federal and state basis. Courts have held, for example, that a state's unfair competition and intellectual property laws cannot provide greater protection than do the federal laws of patent and copyright.[63] In a key case,[64] Chief Justice Warren Burger wrote, "If a State, through a system of protection, were to cause a substantial risk that holders of patentable inventions would not seek patents, but rather would rely on the state protection, we would be compelled to hold that such a system could not constitutionally continue to exist."

Trade secrecy can be selected

Federal patent and copyright laws *do* preempt "equivalent rights," i.e., federal copyright law is the *only* law applicable to the right of authors to control reproduction, and federal patent law is the *only* law granting monopoly rights in an invention. A trade secret violation *could* involve copying, however, and the trade secret misappropriated *could* be for a patentable process. In the case referenced, the Court found it highly unlikely that anyone would abandon the federal protections to choose the "far weaker" state trade secret laws, i.e., the Court upheld the constitutionality of the choice between protective mechanisms. The Court concluded that (in this case) patents and trade secrets could continue to coexist on the basis that the modes of protections were "alternative" (secrecy versus disclosure and dedication). Dedication refers to disclosing the informa-

But once you choose to apply for a patent, trade secrecy disappears

tion to the public in return for a monopoly. You cannot have a monopoly (patent) and restrict disclosure.

Copyright and trade secrecy do not conflict

Since the copyright law mandates deposit, and deposit implies disclosure, there would appear to be a conflict between copyright and trade secret protections. However, the copyright laws, unlike the patent laws, permit the Register to make special exemptions, and the legislative history clearly indicates that copyrights and trade secrets were expected to coexist under these exemptions. Furthermore, deposit is voluntary.

But you could not prevent (only) copying under the trade secrecy laws

The report of the National Commission of New Technological Uses of Copyrighted Works (CONTU), which predated the 1980 copyright revisions, [65] noted, "The availability of copyright for computer programs does not, of course, affect the availability of trade secrets protection. Under the act of 1976 only those state rights that are equivalent to the exclusive granted therein (generally common law copyright) are preempted."

The copying must involve a breach of trust or some other right not protected by copyright

In adopting the current copyright legislation, the Congress clearly intended that copyright protection should not preempt other protections that would apply to the copyrighted material. The scope of federal preemption of state law by the Copyright Act is prescribed by the statute itself: "Nothing in this title annuls or limits any rights or remedies under common law or statutes of any State . . . that are not equivalent to any of the exclusive rights within the general scope of copyright as specified in section 106." What Congress intended by these words is set out in the legislative history of the Act: "The evolving common law rights of 'privacy,' 'publicity,' and trade secrets, . . . would remain unaffected so long as the causes of action contain elements such as invasion of personal rights or a breach of trust or confidentiality. . . ."[66]

Courts have upheld the marriage of copyright and trade secrets. One court[67] noted:

The courts have upheld the use of both trade secrets and copyrights

> It is well settled that copyright protection extends not to the idea itself, but rather to the particular expression used by its author. . . . In contrast, the protection provided by the common law of trade secret misappropriation extends to the very ideas of the author. . . . The practical distinction between the two interests is manifest. . . . The mere fact that an expression is copyrighted does not, in and of itself, disclose the trade secret or eliminate the mantle of confidentiality.

Giving a copyright notice does not imply publication or disclosure

Another stated: "The court is not willing to conclude that . . . affixing a copyright notice . . . voids any claim of secrecy. . . . The statutory copyright notice may be probative of an intent to generally publish, but the court is not willing to conclude . . . that is conclusive proof of publication so as to defeat any claim of secrecy."[68]

Therefore, use both

In summary, you should not only not fear the simultaneous use of copyright and trade secret protections, you should insist on it. What you must do is:

Provide proper notice

1. Provide a simultaneous notice of confidentiality and copyright. See the suggested form given earlier in this chapter or in the preceding chapter.

Don't deposit object code or other confidential material

2. Do not deposit object code for copyright purposes; request an exemption. It is conceivable that a local court could hold that the mere act of depositing confidential material would void a claim of secrecy. If the exemption is denied, deposit the requisite fifty pages of source code *after* insuring that all trade secret information is not included; pad the listing with nonconfidential material if necessary. See Chapter 5 for further explanation and details.

Continue to treat the software as a trade secret

3. Follow all of the other steps related to trade secrets provided earlier in this chapter.

If You Must Go to Court

Planning for a court case can help to avoid one

At this point you should have a fairly good idea of business practices that will help you avoid costly litigation. A brief review of what to consider before you litigate will assist you even further. Of course, if you ever really *do* have to litigate, all of these preparations will be invaluable.

Litigation and anger don't mix

Before you consider litigation you should weigh the disadvantages as well as the advantages. Too frequently litigation is commenced as a result of outrage or a desire for revenge with little or no regard to the consequences. Litigation can result in public embarrassment (even if you win), loss of business relationships, immense contributions of managerial effort, and significant out-of-pocket expense.

A negotiated settlement is often superior to victory in court

Often a negotiated alternative to litigation can provide major benefits (e.g., specific agreement not to recruit other employees). Negotiating a license for the misappropriated trade secret can sometimes be more valuable than a court victory; license agreements frequently provide for competitive restrictions and disclosure of sales, which can provide invaluable market intelligence.

You must demonstrate obligation, failure, and loss

If no alternative exists, you must have a legitimate basis on which to proceed. This *always* involves no less than (1) some obligation by the other party (e.g., an agreement not to compete or not to disclose), (2) a clear failure to satisfy that obligation, and (3) a demonstrable loss as a result of that failure. The weaker your evidence is on any of these three points, the less likely you will be to succeed.

If, for example, there is no written agreement, the first point must be proven in the context of the relationship. As we have seen (and will explore further in the following chapters), this implied relationship can benefit the other party as well as you.

The basis for a trade secret action is set out in the definition adopted by most states:

> One who discloses or uses another's trade secret without any privilege to do so is liable to the other if (a) he discovered the secret by improper means or (b) his disclosure or use constitutes a breach of confidence . . . or (c) he learned of the secret from a third party with notice . . . that it was a secret . . . or (d) he learned the secret with notice . . . that its disclosure was made to him by mistake.[69]

Liability rests on improper or mistaken disclosure after notice

You must establish a relationship of trust or confidence; this can be difficult with third parties

As a *breach* of trust or confidence requires a *relationship* of trust or confidence, no action would succeed against a third party (e.g., an employee of a customer) unless the third party could be shown to have learned the secret in a confidential relationship. This is why it is *so* important that contracts with customers and agents bind them to only disclose the secret in a secondary relationship of confidence. Then, at least, if the third party is acting innocently, a cause of action exists against the original party.

If you can't find the smoking gun you'll have to rely on powder burns such as unnatural costs or lead times,

Your best case will be where the "smoking gun" exists, i.e., where you can establish a clear-cut case of theft. Demonstrating that the other party has copies of restricted trade secret materials would be best. Failing this, you must demonstrate the claim obliquely, i.e., that the other party had access to the secret, that more than "amazing coincidences" exist between the two works, and that the second work was developed in a fraction of the time or cost required for the original. This suggests that accurate records are essential and that hidden identifiers (e.g., intentionally meaningless steps in a program or nonexistent names in a customer or prospect list) can simplify the task of a judge or jury.

Targeted recruiting, or use of a company facility in preparation to compete

If the case involves an employee defecting to a competitor, your case will be far stronger if the employee was recruited to fill a new position (i.e., to take advantage of your trade secrets) than if the employee merely filled an existing opening. It is also very helpful if you can show that the ex-employee used company facilities in preparing to compete (computer time, phones, copiers, marketing information, etc.), as this would clearly constitute a conflict of interest and breach of trust.

Anticipate the defense

(1) Of no secrecy

Due to publicly available components,

The most likely defense you will encounter is that the material in question is not a trade secret at all. A perfect defense would be, in fact, to show that the information was readily available from public sources (e.g., that a customer or prospect list could be derived from a phone book). Your chances as the plaintiff are greatly improved if you can demonstrate that the information is *not* publicly available (e.g., in the case of customer lists, that the information includes a record of buying habits, purchasing authority, etc.) Note also that merely showing that the elements of a claimed trade secret are in the public domain (e.g., names and addresses in a customer list) does not invalidate the claim. Demonstrating that you spent time and money in creating the secret and that it provides a business advantage is the appropriate response.

Copyright deposit,

Or sloppy practices

In the case of software, your adversary might claim that the material has been placed in the public domain by registering and depositing the work for copyright or by unrestricted disclosure to third parties. Adherence to the guidelines previously provided will defeat the first defense, but the second requires a consistency of practices that can stand up to your defendant's "discovery" of facts before a trial and to management's testimony (e.g., "Have you, as Marketing Manager, ever provided the software claimed as a trade secret to a prospect without the prospect knowing and agreeing that it was confidential?").

Of course, your adversary could not on one hand claim that the material in question was not a trade secret and then treat it as one internally. In fact, if you can show that the appropriating party is distributing the material (e.g., the software) only under nondisclosure agreements or restricted licensing agreements, you are a long way toward defeating this defense. Remember, however, that a court could find that despite these protections by the defendant the material is in the public domain as a result of your sloppy practices; in other words, you both could lose.

(2) Of employee rights to the secret

A second defense could be the claim that the material is the property of a departing employee, i.e., that the employee knew the trade secret at the time of employment, would have learned it in other equivalent employment, or that, in the absence of an agreement specifically related to the material, it is the employee's and not the company's property. This defense is best defeated by (1) requiring incoming employees to make or waive any trade secret claims at the time of hire, and (2) clear, written, employment conditions agreed to at the time of hire, and renewed regularly.

Or (3) of reverse engineering

The defense of "reverse engineering" is another acceptable trade secret defense, but the circumstances must support the claim. Showing that a new product was produced with the services of a former employee at lower cost or in a shorter time than would otherwise have been possible will defeat such defense. Accurate records are obviously essential.

You will probably want an injunction

Injunctive relief is usually limited to a narrowly defined market, geography, and time period

You will most likely be seeking an injunction if you must go to court. Courts tend to be very reluctant to issue injunctions that restrict a business's ability to compete or an individual's ability to seek employment. Accordingly, requests for injunctive relief should be as narrowly drawn as possible. A court will want to limit an injunction to a subset of an industry or to a geographic area where direct competition would be damaging. Broad injunctions that provide blanket restrictions on the use of the subject matter or that cover an entire industry are rarely granted. If you are the only one in an industry with a specific process, product, or result based on a trade secret, the injunction will be much easier to get.[70] Injunctive relief will generally be limited to the competitive "head start" the secret provides, i.e., how long it would take (or did take) to develop it independently.[71]

Conclusion

As in war, litigation winners are also losers

Planning for trade secrets litigation is a little like planning for a war; focusing on the costs of battle can frequently lead to peaceful resolutions of conflict. In addition, a strong defense can deter aggression. When a trade secrecy claim involves an ex-employee, the employer always loses, even if the case is won. Not only is a valuable employee gone, but so are significant expenditures on legal fees and executive time. If the case is lost, a new, enraged, and competent competitor may add to the costs. Additional employees may decide to follow either the departee or the lesson provided.

Trade secrecy and employee relations are one subject

For all these reasons, good employee relations and a rigorous trade secrecy program must go hand in hand. Employers also need to know and respect the rights of their employees, rights that are more and more frequently statutory. This is our next topic.

7 EMPLOYEE RELATIONS

Introduction

What are the rights of the employees who are paid to develop, enhance, or support your confidential information or trade secrets—especially the software? What right does someone from your sales force have to use your customer and prospect lists in subsequent employment? What right do you have to suppress competition that arises when ex-employees convert the valuable training you provide into a new business?

Until recently, public policy favored management

Until recently there was little to debate; management practices and public policy both favored the rights of the employer over those of the employee. Because the employer paid for the employee's services, the employer had an absolute right to the employee's output. The employee, by accepting the job, gave up many of the rights of an individual working alone, especially those rights relating to inventions and the development of trade secrets.

**The rules
have changed**

**Increasing conflicts
between employers
and their employees**

**Until recently,
employers chose not
to fight**

**The "new" definition
of rights requires a
different management
approach**

**. . . Which parallels
the shift toward a
more open
management style**

All this has changed. Worker mobility has increased, raising issues that would have rarely surfaced in earlier times. Courts have rapidly replaced the old pro-management view with one that attempts to balance the competing rights of corporations and individual workers. State legislatures have followed suit, regulating the rights of workers and, in some cases, banning practices that were once routine (e.g., covenants not to compete with the employer).

The result has been a dramatic increase in the number of conflicts between employees and their former employer. Most of these cases involve competition by the ex-employee which the employer considers to be unfair, frequently centering on trade secrets and other confidential information (especially software and customer lists) that both parties claim as theirs. The tremendous growth in venture capital to fund start-ups, particularly in high-technology areas, has fueled the fire.

Employers have been slow to react. The common view appears to be that there is little that can be done, the pendulum having swung completely to the side of the employee. The competitive losses that result from new businesses spawned by ex-employees are frequently treated as ordinary business risks, even when the ex-employees take unfair advantage of their former employer. Few companies have been willing to expose themselves to the unfavorable publicity that surrounds a large organization pursuing a few entrepreneurial employees. Worse, only a few companies have adopted internal business practices and procedures that would stand the scrutiny of the public and the courts.

This is the real issue and subject of this chapter. Management rights have not disappeared, they have simply been more clearly defined. This demands new practices and procedures that recognize the rights as well as the obligations of the employee, along with the rights and obligations of management.

Happily, the shift in public policy relating to employee rights coincides with other changes in management theory concerning employee relations. Consensus management demands greater communication, understanding, and trust between the employer and the employee, which in turn means more precise definitions of respective rights and obligations. Simultaneously, the worldwide shortage of programmers and system engineers has forced a review of the employer's ability to compete for their skills, including the elimination of unnecessarily restrictive employment conditions.

A program that balances the rights of employees and the employer should start with a clear understanding of the legal rights of the worker, which is our next topic.

Employee Rights

Skills brought to the job or available through competitive employment belong to the employee

Some of the "new" rights of an employee seem, in retrospect, obvious. Yet it is amazing how many companies still act as if they are battling with their employees and an overly liberal society on every issue. For example, an employee has an unqualified right to the skills brought to the job, including any trade secrets legitimately acquired in prior employment. These skills, and also those skills gained on the job that the employee would have gained in a competitive position, cannot be restricted by the employer. Furthermore, if an employee develops a trade secret using these skills, absent a contractual agreement to the contrary, the employee may be free to use the new secret in future employment.

Employers don't have an automatic right to the inventions made by employees

In general, an employee has a right to developments made as a product of his or her skill when the employer has not contributed information, expenses, or supervision beyond normal job-related levels. In summary, and logically, unless you hire someone to invent, you don't have an automatic right to their inventions simply because you are the employer. You can change this by mutual agreement, but there must be some consideration given in exchange for the transferred right (e.g., a raise, promotion, etc).

Protection of secrets requires agreement

Similarly, without a written agreement, when an employer discloses something to his or her employees it will be considered to be a trade secret only if its secrecy would have been evident from either the way the disclosure was made or from the competitive environment. Even when an agreement exists, however, general information and training that an employee would have received in equivalent employment elsewhere belongs to the employee. This right extends to trade secrets developed by the employee that are part of the employee's general skill and knowledge.[72]

State law may govern employee rights in trade secrets and inventions

Certain states, most notably California, have established tests that attempt to balance the employer's need to protect a trade secret against the employee's rights in seeking the most desirable employment possible.[73]

California has also legislated an employee's rights to inventions made on his or her own time, without the use of company facilities or property. Even in states without specific legislation on this subject, the judicial trend has been similar. The following general rules closely parallel most court rulings on the subject and state laws where they exist:

1. Discoveries made by an employee who was hired to invent and that are within the scope of the assigned work will generally belong to the employer.

2. Discoveries made using the employer's resources by an employee who was not hired to invent or that fall outside of the area of assigned work will generally belong to the employee, but the employer will have a "shop right" to use the invention.

3. Discoveries made without the use of the employer's resources or trade secrets and outside of the employee's assigned duties will generally belong to the employee.

Noncompete agreements are either illegal or difficult to enforce

Post-employment agreements not to compete or disclose trade secrets are also under increasing scrutiny by the courts and state legislatures. California has once again set an example by outlawing *any* post-employment restrictions on employee mobility. The trend is clearly counter to the previously common practice of requiring broad noncompete agreements from every employee. Even in states without legislative prohibitions, case law is overwhelmingly against noncompete agreements that are not limited with respect to industry, geography, and duration. Such agreements, even when narrowly drawn, have been enforceable only when it would obviously be difficult for an employee to separate trade secret information from its use in the new employment.

Apparent breaches of trust may not be

When employees go into direct competition with a former employer, a breach of trust does not necessarily result. Courts have found it permissible, for example, for employees to arrange financing, develop marketing plans, and even sign leases and hire others in the anticipation of competing with their employer, so long as it is done on their own time and expense and does not involve the use of the employer's resources. It would also be legally permissible for the soon-to-defect employees to use general business information in their planning, no matter how specialized within an industry, such as supply sources, market information, and promotional techniques, so long as specific trade secrets of the employer were not misappropriated.

To summarize, even when a written agreement exists to the contrary, an employee will have a right to:

A summary

information brought to the job and information subsequently learned that could have been learned elsewhere

inventions or discoveries made without the use of company resources

subsequent employment anywhere, even with a direct competitor, so long as company property (e.g., trade secrets) is not compromised

plan to leave an employer while still employed, even to actively organize to go into competition, so long as company resources and property are not used in the process.

Rights of Employers: Are There Any Left?

Many rights of the employer remain

Is the deck stacked against the employer? Not really. An employer still has significant legal and moral rights in the property his or her shareholders pay to develop, and courts are increasingly recognizing software as one of these valuable intangible rights.

"Lost" rights aren't really lost

Consider agreements not to compete. It is true that these are now patently illegal in certain jurisdictions and difficult to enforce in all others. Is this a major loss to the employer? I think not. The employer's interest is in protecting property, not in restricting employee movement. The inability of an employer to dictate where an employee may or may not work actually increases the employee's obligations to protect the trade secrets and confidential information of the former employer. Written agreements that cover confidential information can be far broader than noncompete or trade secret protections, and a court is more likely to be sympathetic to a claim that a specific job, by its very nature, forces a disclosure of trade secrets or confidential information than it would be to a claim that simply working for a competitor is "unfair."

But much clearer definitions of mutual obligations are required

Similarly, employers should not have any great interest in inventions made by employees on their own time that do not relate to their work. A blanket assignment to the employer of all rights in any inventions made by the employee was used in the past because it was easier to draft and was thought to be easier to enforce, but this is no longer true. Legislative and judicial invalidation of such agreements has really not reduced the employer's property rights, however; it has merely shifted the burden, requiring a clearer definition of the rights of the employee or employer whenever both parties might otherwise have a claim in the same information or material.

Better management is the key

Simply put, the new burden on managers is to do their jobs better. This means spelling out the conditions applicable to a job clearly and fairly before the employee signs on. It means documenting for the record and for the employee all disclosures of confidential and trade secret information. It means monitoring company investments in new research and development to insure that the collective efforts of a project team do not subsequently appear to be the invention of an individual. It also means constantly reinforcing the obligations of the employee (and the company) in the protection of intangible assets.

Highly Recommended: A Handbook of Business Practices

A rigorous program to protect intangible assets need not be offensive to your employees. In fact, it can and should be a natural part of the corporate culture and its management practices. One of the best approaches is to use a "Handbook of Business Conduct and Practices" to set forth all of the obligations, rights, and accepted practices of employees. Obviously, this Handbook can cover more issues than those related to trade secrets and confidential information (e.g., gifts from suppliers, nondiscrimination policies, and the like). For purposes of protecting intangible assets, however, its very existence can be invaluable.

A contract between the company and its employees

With prior consent from both parties, the Handbook can constitute a contract. It can and should, for example, be made freely available to job applicants, with the clear understanding that the terms will apply to any employment offer. The potential employee would then acknowledge acceptance of these terms in a signed application for employment. Once hired, the company should regularly remind the employee of the obligations agreed to. This is frequently done by asking the employee to review the Handbook once a year and to reconfirm agreement with its terms by signing a confirmation card. The problem with this approach is that no "consideration" has been given by management (other than continued employment, which may not be enough) if the terms have changed.

Renewed at every career change

And performance review

A preferable approach is to make reconfirmation of the agreement, with the latest terms and conditions of employment, a prerequisite to all raises and promotions. The benefits of this approach are: (1) the procedural aspects are straightforward, as the reconfirmation can be included in the salary change or promotion form signed by the employee and the manager; (2) the employee is made aware that the conditions of the new job may be more stringent than those of the previous job; (3) the consideration given is explicit and therefore more palatable than a unilateral demand from management; and (4) a company representative, the employee's manager, is involved and can therefore intercept any concerns, misunderstandings, or resentment at the earliest possible time.

Managers must understand their own policies

Another advantage of a Handbook is the discipline it forces on management. As it must be written for the lowest-level employee, all legal mumbo-jumbo must be eliminated. As it will be widely circulated within the company (and possibly outside), management must not only be conversant with the terms and conditions of employment but be willing and able to explain and defend them. If nothing else, this will improve management's ability to defend the practices and policies should a court challenge ever arise. More important, however, it will insure that silly or discriminatory practices are purged or modified *before* a court pronounces them as such. Note, however, that while the Handbook can be an agreement between the company and the employee on mutual rights and obligations, *specific* information is not protected unless and until it is exchanged with the knowledge and agreement of both parties that it is privileged.

What the Handbook Should Contain

Philosophy

Given the importance of a Handbook of Business Conduct and Practices, the following topics should be addressed:

1. Include a direct opening statement of the business's philosophy, especially its ethical posture. For example:

   We're in business to make money honestly and fairly. Our employees, customers, and shareholders all benefit from adherence to this philosophy. This book summarizes rules for collective and individual behavior that will achieve this objective. We expect employees and their management to understand and adhere to these rules; we believe in them so strongly as to have made them a condition of all employment.

Agreement

2. Include a reminder of the employee's contract(s) with the company. For example:

   As a new employee you were recruited to fill a position of trust and responsibility in part because you shared the Company's philosophy and agreed to the conditions of employment as set out in this Handbook, including those related to the protection of the Company's confidential information and trade secrets, the ownership of inventions, and the like. As your career with the Company progresses, you may be offered the opportunity to work with increasingly sensitive or valuable information. In these cases, even more specific understandings may be required, but they would supplement rather than replace the practices and procedures that follow.

Items covered

3. Describe the intangible assets to be protected, and how to protect them. For example:

   The Company's assets include many that are intangible, e.g., know-how, software, ideas, technologies, concepts, designs, copyrights, strategies, product plans, and prospect/customer lists. Every employee must assist in protecting these assets as their loss would damage the Company's shareholders, customers, and employees. Any misappropriation of these assets is theft, and it will be treated as such. Even inadvertent disclosure of the Company's confidential information could cause irreparable damage. Accordingly, employees must never remove materials that they believe to be confidential from protected areas without prior permission and must return all confidential materials to a secure area once finished with them. Each department has procedures for the handling of confidential information which every employee must understand and adhere to. It is a breach of the trust granted by the Company and fellow employees for any employee to discuss or otherwise disclose confidential information to third parties without explicit approval.

It may be required that the Company and its employees, as a normal course of our business, receive or be exposed to the confidential information or trade secrets of our customers and suppliers. In such instances, you must protect this information as if it belonged to the Company, according to the practices and policies set out in this Handbook.

Who owns what

4. Make ownership of inventions clear. For example:

Anything unrelated to your job that you invent, write, or develop on your own time without Company resources is your property. Anything that you invent, write, or develop on Company time or using Company resources (including confidential information, company facilities, computer time, etc.) belongs to the Company, whether or not it relates to your job. Any inventions, developments, or writings that we pay you to make, i.e., that are a logical part of your assignment, belong to the Company, regardless of the other Company resources applied. You agreed to these terms and to assist in perfecting the Company's title in any inventions, developments, or writings as a condition of your original employment and as a condition of any intervening status changes; please discuss them with your manager if any specific case is unclear.

Preexisting conditions

5. Make any preexisting conditions clear before hiring or promoting someone. For example:

Job applicants who believe they possess trade secrets or confidential information that could restrict the Company's ability to use their talents to the fullest or compromise the rights of others must disclose that fact to the Company in advance. Similarly, any inventions, designs, or writings of the applicant that are to be excluded from the terms of employment must be agreed to in advance. Unless disclosed to the Company in advance, the job applicant takes complete responsibility for any breach of trust or loss of rights that might occur as a result of employment by the Company.

Obligations of departing employees

6. Specify termination procedures and obligations. For example:

Terminating employees have a continuing obligation to the Company. In accepting a position that involved exposure to the Company's confidential information and trade secrets, the employee agreed to protect this information during and beyond the term of employment. The Company is not interested in restricting an employee's future mobility, but certain natural restrictions may arise out of the Company's disclosures, e.g., accepting a directly competitive job in which the use of Company confidential information could not be avoided may constitute a breach of trust. Employees are expected to weigh the advantages and disadvantages of accepting a Company job or promotion offer in advance, with special emphasis on the obligations of trust that might survive employment with the Company. Upon termination, the employee will be reminded of these obligations. As the Company will react strongly to a breach of trust, employees should seek advice before accepting a position outside of the company that might compromise these obligations.

Terminating employees must return all Company property and confidential materials to the Company, including any handwritten notes or notebooks that relate to confidential information. The terminating employee will be asked to acknowledge the return of all such materials in writing.

Other items for the handbook

You might also want to include these other items, unrelated to the protection of intangible assets:

7. Moonlighting
8. Political activities
9. Stock ownership in suppliers or competitors
10. Giving and accepting gifts
11. Using "insider information" for personal financial gain
12. Acceptable competitive practices
13. Illegal practices, e.g.:
    a. antitrust violations
    b. discrimination
    c. misappropriation of customer or competitive information/property
14. Prohibitions on post-employment recruiting of company employees.

There are, of course, many other topics that you may choose to include. The important point to remember is that this one document can and should establish the operating philosophy you expect your management and employees to follow. Don't be afraid to be blunt; if the operating philosophy is good and the rules fair, they will be perceived as such.

Special Treatment for Special Employees

Clerical workers cannot be held to the same standards

Instituting a formal management procedure to reinforce the company's rules and procedures vis-a-vis trade secrets and confidential information each time an employee is hired or promoted also allows custom tailoring of the program to the job. While it is reasonable to demand that clerical workers protect confidential information that might come into their possession, that is probably all that is reasonable. Employees working in especially sensitive areas, however, for example those who are hired to invent or develop trade secrets, can be asked to sign supplemental agreements that specifically identify the materials and information considered sensitive and the procedures for handling it.

Notebooks are a special case

A special example is the treatment of employee notebooks. In ordinary cases, an employee's notebooks would be considered personal property whether or not trade secret or confidential information was recorded in them. The notebooks of employees who are *not* engaged in the development of confidential information or trade secrets would have such information only through other (presumably prohibited and probably illegal) means, but employees hired to develop such material would have that information legitimately.

Accordingly, it is a good practice to have employees who are hired to invent agree in advance that any notes made during the course of employment relating to the company's trade secrets or confidential information are the company's property.

A second important reason to have supplemental agreements with key employees is to itemize *specific* trade secrets and other confidential information to which they will be exposed. This is *very* useful, as it establishes a basis of trust and understanding with respect to specific information at the time of employment or promotion that would weaken any subsequent claim of inadequate notice and consideration or of unilateral restrictions on future employment. Simultaneously, and to the benefit of both parties, you can itemize and exclude specific trade secret information that the employee brings to the job. It is a good practice to provide for this exclusion in all employment agreements and to include the topic in all job interviews.

For key employees noncompete agreements, despite the enforcement difficulties, can be useful

As key employees can be held to far more stringent standards than can clerical workers, in special cases narrowly drawn noncompete agreements may be a useful supplement to the more broadly applicable agreements on confidential information and trade secrets. As previously noted, these agreements are legally void in some jurisdictions and hard to enforce in others. Nevertheless, they are *very* useful in letting employees know what the company considers to be "unfair" and, if very specific, may be enforceable, especially if directly linked to the employee's obligations not to disclose confidential information or trade secrets.

The important considerations in a noncompete agreement are (1) it should be for a short period of time, e.g., one year; (2) it should specify the lowest level of prohibited activity possible, preferably *naming* specific competitors, software, and/or geographic areas; and (3) it should be severable from all other agreements, i.e., any finding that the noncompetition agreement is not enforceable should not jeopardize any other agreements with the employee.

Adequate consideration is required

As with all other employment terms, noncompete agreements require adequate consideration in exchange for the rights waived. This in turn dictates that noncompete covenants be a condition of the job, to be formally accepted *prior* to employment or promotion.

"Selling" noncompete and other special agreements that supplement the Handbook to key employees is a critical management task that is made much easier if the terms are reasonable and known in advance. In some cases, especially after an acquisition, a wholesale change in practices may preclude the more orderly and understandable progression in an employee's career. This is a major item being overlooked in most acquisitions and mergers that involve valuable intangible assets. Not only are the qualities of the assets not being adequately researched but the potential impact on the employee population of a change in practices can be extreme.

Acquisitions and Mergers: A Special Problem

Preexisting conditions can be difficult or impossible to reverse

Typically, employees become suspicious during any change in organizational structure or ownership, and those contemplating career changes are far more vulnerable to pressures to leave (including paranoia about management's "true" intentions). There is very little that the surviving or new management can do in such a situation if the employee agreements to protect information or trade secrets are inadequate. Any move to demand stronger agreements would run precisely counter to management's normal tendency to be accommodating, and, additional considerations aside, the employee's real or perceived loss of rights can cause problems.

Your only option may be to walk away

The right solution is to solve the problem of asset protection *before* an acquisition, either by simply not acquiring a company with inadequate procedures or requiring that they be fixed first. If the target company's intangible assets are large, there may be other good reasons for backing away from the deal. If the potential exists for a loss of those assets through imperfect title, misappropriation, or mass defections of key employees, the value ascribed to the transaction may change dramatically, yet this issue is rarely examined rigorously in pre-acquisition "due diligence."

Set aside enough

To tie it in a bundle

If you decide to go ahead, make sure that adequate costs have been set aside to implement the asset protection program positively. For example, your program might involve organizing a campaign to sell the whole new package of benefits and practices to the new employees. If this package isn't better than what it was before, you may have to ante up. If your existing program to protect company information and trade secrets is reasonable, you will probably want to insist that every new employee be covered. Even if you do your best at selling the program, tie it to increased benefits, increased pay, or whatever, you will experience defections. This should also be part of your pre-acquisition integration plan; the cost of these defections and the threat they might represent should not be minimized.

Costs are always under-estimated

It is almost always true that the cost of an acquisition, especially post-acquisition integration, is far more than management estimated in the passion of purchase. I therefore recommend that every potential acquirer add the following questions to the pre-acquisition checklist:

1. Are the company's intangible assets protected to our existing standards? If not, what is our exposure to a total loss of these assets (e.g., if trade secrets turn out to be in the public domain)?

2. What level of expense will be required to convince the maximum number of new employees to accept our standard terms and conditions of employment?

3. In the event of (inevitable) defections, what is our exposure to the new competition that might result? If unfair, could we prove it and at what cost?

Other Practices Worth Noting

Restrict access to those with "a need to know"

In protecting trade secrets and confidential information it is essential that the recipient be notified that the material is privileged. This is especially important for your employees. It is not uncommon, however, for *very* sensitive information (e.g., the source programs for software treated as a trade secret) to be generally available to employees. This is a major management error. Trade secret information must be restricted to those with a "need to know," even among employees.

"Company confidential" labels are important

Establish labeling rules

Another major management error is presuming that the "confidential" label need be applied only when information might be subject to outside scrutiny. An employee's claim that he or she had easy access to information that did not contain any warnings as to its privileged nature might defeat a subsequent claim by management that it was a breach of trust for the employee to use that information in subsequent employment. Don't indiscriminately stamp everything, however. Capricious use of "confidential" labels could also help defeat trade secrecy claims. Put them where they really count. This would include, for example, modifying any library maintenance routines to display a warning whenever the program was accessed or printed. In the case of printed output, this should be *at least* on every other page of a continuous listing.

Restrict and log access

Restrict access to confidential information. Make sure that your programming areas are secure, and log every instance of an employee signing out confidential information. Have the employee counter-sign the log.

Conduct regular training

Conduct regular employee training sessions concerning confidential information. Make the meetings interactive (e.g., ask for employees to hypothesize ways that the company's confidential information could be compromised and to suggest counter strategies). This has a dual effect: It keeps your practices strong and it insures that every employee knows the rules.

Document investments

For all development projects, keep a log of who was assigned to the work and what, if any, preexisting trade secrets or special company facilities were contributed to the project. This may be an invaluable record if an employee were to subsequently claim the output as personal property.

Certify compliance

Add a briefing on the employee's obligations concerning privileged information to every management review. Require management and employee acknowledgment that procedures have been explained and are being adhered to.

Remind departing employees of their obligations

Send a letter to every terminating employee who had access to confidential information reminding them of their continuing obligations to that information. *Do not* try to intimidate the ex-employee; this technique will only backfire. Simply remind the employee of his or her commitments to the company and the importance of the information to the company's economic health. In those instances when an employee goes to work for a competitor, send a copy of the termination letter to the new employer. Once again, be positive and do not threaten; unless you have clear evidence of a breach of trust, your actions could be taken as attempting to restrict the employee's mobility. Fair notice of a contractual relationship is a good idea, however.

Be careful

Everything we have covered thus far has been in an attempt to avoid conflict. When you do have to seek legal redress, however, be sure all your ducks are on the pond before you open fire. Few things will harm management's credibility more than attacks on ex-employees that appear to be either vindictive or simply a demonstration of power.

Don't go to court without an airtight case

Legal action is only recommended if you have a "smoking gun" (evidence that an employee used company facilities in preparing to compete, stole company trade secrets, or was recruited to a new position simply to duplicate proprietary work). If you have followed the procedures suggested, such evidence may be easier to demonstrate than it sounds. Seek a temporary injunction that is narrowly limited to the subject matter at hand (e.g., to prevent the use of specific confidential material in the development of specific competitive offerings within a specific industry). Be prepared to demonstrate the investment you have made in the subject matter and the economic advantage it provides.

But go if you can win

Do go to court if you have a case; management's unwillingness to prosecute even the most blatant misappropriation of company property has contributed to the recent explosion in such cases. Well-publicized recent victories by IBM and others against ex-employees who misappropriated company trade secrets have put their employees on notice that the company management will be fair but rigorous in defending company property. This is the message you want to convey, without going to court if possible, but doing so if necessary.

Summary and Conclusion

Most of the problems related to employee misappropriation of confidential information do not arise out of venal motives. Rather, they are the result of missed communications, poorly defined responsibilities, and sloppy management practices. Employees will generally behave responsibly when told the rules in advance and when there is peer pressure to act in the best interest of the enterprise. These same honest employees will casually or willfully disregard rules or procedures that are not part of the business ethic or that are not respected and enforced by the business's management. For this reason, a company's asset protection program must start at the top, be ingrained in day-to-day operations, and make sense to all concerned.

8 CUSTOMER CONTRACTS

Introduction

There are three types of software transactions

In the provision of software products or services there are generally three types of relationships between the vendor and the customer:

1. The vendor develops custom software for the customer.
2. The vendor licenses standard software to the customer under specific restrictive conditions.
3. The vendor sells a copy of the software to the customer in a "retail" transaction, usually through an independent distribution chain.

Only two of the three involve a contract

There has been considerable confusion on these important distinctions in the marketplace, even by those closest to the business. Only the first two categories lend themselves to a contractual relationship at the time of the transaction. The first category, custom de-

97

velopment, usually involves a specialized contract, while the second, direct licensing of software by the author, is generally done under a standardized agreement. The retail transaction is a relatively new way of marketing software and, from the standpoint of contractual protections, the most problematic.

Retail Transactions and the Law

A "sale" implies a transfer of rights in the underlying property. In many cases, even if the parties agree, these rights cannot be abridged. "Sales" also may force warranty obligations and liabilities on the vendor, as a matter of law. Every state except Louisiana has, for example, adopted the Uniform Commercial Code (UCC), which regulates commercial transactions.

Under the Uniform Commercial Code, any "goods" that are "sold" are subject to implied warranties unless waived by both parties. Sales of software have been held to fall under the UCC's jurisdiction.[74] Licenses of software, however, which convey only a limited "right to use," will generally be treated differently under the law.

As only an *intangible* right is involved when software is licensed (see Chapter 2), laws applicable to real and personal property sales (e.g., the UCC, "consumer protection" laws, implied product warranties, sales and excise taxes on transfers of personal property, etc.) generally do not apply. (Be cautious with respect to taxes, however, as several states have recognized the value of software license transactions in special tax legislation).

When a transaction *is* subject to the UCC, if (1) you know what the customer is going to use your product for, and (2) the customer is relying on your skill to furnish a product to fill that need, "implied warranties of fitness and merchantability for a particular purpose" will generally apply. These implicit warranties can be waived, but only if both parties agree in writing. Even if formally waived, however, and despite contractual prohibitions on verbal amendments, courts have held that verbal promises made by agents and employees can amend a retail contract.

In addition to the UCC, there is a body of case law applicable to the sale of goods. These decisions generally support the right of the new "owner" to do anything legal with his or her property, despite restrictions in the sale agreement. This is especially important to the software vendor with trade secrets or confidential information to protect.

Last but not least in the list of problems (for the seller) resulting from the retail sale of goods are state consumer protection laws that may also govern the extent to which a seller can disclaim warranties and service obligations. While these laws differ from state to state, it is safe to say that the buyer of goods that are defective or cause damage will generally have a variety of local remedies to pursue.

Retail sales do not involve contracts

In fact, in this chapter on customer contracts there is little to be said about retail transactions, other than to point out the futility of trying to force a contractual relationship between the parties at the time of sale. There are, however, ways that post-sale relationships can be established to change the relationship with the customer.

License Agreements and the Law

Service contracts and licenses of intangible rights are generally not treated as a "sale" of "goods" under either the UCC or the case law governing retail transactions. In addition, where the body of case law would support the thesis that usage restrictions are largely unenforceable after a sale, just the opposite is the case under an explicit license to use something. For these reasons, most software vendors try to characterize their transactions as "licenses" versus "sales." In addition, to limit their liability for verbal commitments, most software vendors restrict the authority of their dealers, agents, and distributors.

"Caveat emptor" still applies in commercial contracts

Since most license transactions are between commercial enterprises, a court will generally hold the buyer to a higher standard of competence than it would a less-sophisticated consumer. The result is that the contract rules. Both parties are expected to have a thorough understanding of any restrictive covenants or waivers of rights. Thus, while it is generally impossible to waive implied warranties of "merchantability and fitness for a specific purpose" or to disclaim liability for ordinary damages in sales to consumers, a different standard applies when both parties are corporations that presumably have access to competent counsel.

The Objective of a Contract

Preventing copying and disclosure is the goal

Regardless of the type of transaction, from an asset protection standpoint the objective of any agreement with a customer is to prevent unauthorized copying and, when trade secrets are involved, disclosure. Even though unauthorized copying is a violation of federal law (see Chapter 5), a contract or licensing agreement establishes the basis for a civil suit should the contract be breached, even if no trade secrets are involved. With respect to trade secrets where no federal law applies, the contract is the *only* means of protection available. Last, but certainly not least, contracts are *the* internationally respected way of regulating commercial transactions.

Form contracts are available

I do not intend for this book to be your guide to software contracting, nor do I intend it to be a substitute for legal counsel. Rather, we will explore software protection concepts and mechanisms that you will want to consider or avoid in developing your own contracts. If you want form contracts to work from, the Association of Data Processing Service Organizations (ADAPSO) provides an excellent set that covers nearly every type of data processing transaction.[75]

Key items in asset protection

There are four essential items to be covered in agreements related to the protection of assets:

1. Ownership
2. Transfer of copyrights
3. Protection of confidential information
4. Remedies

Without a contract, ownership transfers in the sale, copyrights remain with the author, there is no confidentiality obligation, and the remedies are as provided in the statutes. In short, there is no agreement between the parties that can be breached. We will examine how and why a contractual relationship should be structured with relation to all four elements, but first let's look at the no-contract situation, e.g., the retail sale.

The Retail Sale

Question: What are the rights of a buyer?

When you buy a book are you under any special obligations? "Of course," you say, "I cannot copy it except for 'fair use' purposes." But what if the book's flyleaf said that the book was sold subject to your waiving any rights to resell it, to loan it to someone else, or to use any of the ideas it contains? "Nonsense" is your probable reply, and you're right.

International Business Machines Corporation   Boca Raton, Florida 33432

IBM Program License Agreement

YOU SHOULD CAREFULLY READ THE FOLLOWING TERMS AND CONDITIONS BEFORE OPENING THIS DISKETTE PACKAGE. OPENING THIS DISKETTE PACKAGE INDICATES YOUR ACCEPTANCE OF THESE TERMS AND CONDITIONS. IF YOU DO NOT AGREE WITH THEM, YOU SHOULD PROMPTLY RETURN THE PACKAGE UNOPENED; AND YOUR MONEY WILL BE REFUNDED.

IBM provides this program and licenses its use in the United States and Puerto Rico. You assume responsibility for the selection of the program to achieve your intended results, and for the installation, use and results obtained from the program.

LICENSE

You may:

a. use the program on a single machine;

b. copy the program into any machine readable or printed form for backup or modification purposes in support of your use of the program on the single machine (Certain programs, however, may include mechanisms to limit or inhibit copying. They are marked "copy protected.");

c. modify the program and/or merge it into another program for your use on the single machine (Any portion of this program merged into another program will continue to be subject to the terms and conditions of this Agreement.); and,

d. transfer the program and license to another party if the other party agrees to accept the terms and conditions of this Agreement. If you transfer the program, you must at the same time either transfer all copies whether in printed or machine-readable form to the same party or destroy any copies not transferred; this includes all modifications and portions of the program contained or merged into other programs.

You must reproduce and include the copyright notice on any copy, modification or portion merged into another program.

YOU MAY NOT USE, COPY, MODIFY, OR TRANSFER THE PROGRAM, OR ANY COPY, MODIFICATION OR MERGED PORTION, IN WHOLE OR IN PART, EXCEPT AS EXPRESSLY PROVIDED FOR IN THIS LICENSE.

IF YOU TRANSFER POSSESSION OF ANY COPY, MODIFICATION OR MERGED PORTION OF THE PROGRAM TO ANOTHER PARTY, YOUR LICENSE IS AUTOMATICALLY TERMINATED.

TERM

The license is effective until terminated. You may terminate it at any other time by destroying the program together with all copies, modifications and merged portions in any form. It will also terminate upon conditions set forth elsewhere in this Agreement or if you fail to comply with any term or condition of this Agreement. You agree upon such termination to destroy the program together with all copies, modifications and merged portions in any form.

LIMITED WARRANTY

THE PROGRAM IS PROVIDED "AS IS" WITHOUT WARRANTY OF ANY KIND, EITHER EXPRESSED OR IMPLIED, INCLUDING, BUT NOT LIMITED TO THE IMPLIED WARRANTIES OF MERCHANTABILITY AND FITNESS FOR A PARTICULAR PURPOSE. THE ENTIRE RISK AS TO THE QUALITY AND PERFORMANCE OF THE PROGRAM IS WITH YOU. SHOULD THE PROGRAM PROVE DEFECTIVE, YOU (AND NOT IBM OR AN AUTHORIZED PERSONAL COMPUTER DEALER) ASSUME THE ENTIRE COST OF ALL NECESSARY SERVICING, REPAIR OR CORRECTION.

SOME STATES DO NOT ALLOW THE EXCLUSION OF IMPLIED WARRANTIES, SO THE ABOVE EXCLUSION MAY NOT APPLY TO YOU. THIS WARRANTY GIVES YOU SPECIFIC LEGAL RIGHTS AND YOU MAY ALSO HAVE OTHER RIGHTS WHICH VARY FROM STATE TO STATE.

IBM does not warrant that the functions contained in the program will meet your requirements or that the operation of the program will be uninterrupted or error free.

However, IBM warrants the diskette(s) or cassettes on which the program is furnished, to be free from defects in materials and workmanship under normal use for a period of ninety (90) days from the date of delivery to you as evidenced by a copy of your receipt.

LIMITATIONS OF REMEDIES

IBM's entire liability and your exclusive remedy shall be:

1. the replacement of any diskette or cassette not meeting IBM's "Limited Warranty" and which is returned to IBM or an authorized IBM PERSONAL COMPUTER dealer with a copy of your receipt, or

2. if IBM or the dealer is unable to deliver a replacement diskette or cassette which is free of defects in materials or workmanship, you may terminate this Agreement by returning the program and your money will be refunded.

IN NO EVENT WILL IBM BE LIABLE TO YOU FOR ANY DAMAGES, INCLUDING ANY LOST PROFITS, LOST SAVINGS OR OTHER INCIDENTAL OR CONSEQUENTIAL DAMAGES ARISING OUT OF THE USE OR INABILITY TO USE SUCH PROGRAM EVEN IF IBM OR AN AUTHORIZED IBM PERSONAL COMPUTER DEALER HAS BEEN ADVISED OF THE POSSIBILITY OF SUCH DAMAGES, OR FOR ANY CLAIM BY ANY OTHER PARTY.

SOME STATES DO NOT ALLOW THE LIMITATION OR EXCLUSION OF LIABILITY FOR INCIDENTAL OR CONSEQUENTIAL DAMAGES SO THE ABOVE LIMITATION OR EXCLUSION MAY NOT APPLY TO YOU.

GENERAL

You may not sublicense, assign or transfer the license or the program except as expressly provided in this Agreement. Any attempt otherwise to sublicense, assign or transfer any of the rights, duties or obligations hereunder is void.

This Agreement will be governed by the laws of the State of Florida.

Should you have any questions concerning this Agreement, you may contact IBM by writing to IBM Personal Computer, Sales and Service, P.O. Box 1328-W Boca Raton, Florida 33432.

YOU ACKNOWLEDGE THAT YOU HAVE READ THIS AGREEMENT, UNDERSTAND IT AND AGREE TO BE BOUND BY ITS TERMS AND CONDITIONS. YOU FURTHER AGREE THAT IT IS THE COMPLETE AND EXCLUSIVE STATEMENT OF THE AGREEMENT BETWEEN US WHICH SUPERCEDES ANY PROPOSAL OR PRIOR AGREEMENT, ORAL OR WRITTEN, AND ANY OTHER COMMUNICATIONS BETWEEN US RELATING TO THE SUBJECT MATTER OF THIS AGREEMENT.

6172208

FIGURE 8.1   IBM Program License Agreement

Answer: To do anything not proscribed by law

The common-sense logic that says you can do anything you want with property you purchase, so long as you do not break the law, is generally true; transferring restrictive covenants in commercial transactions involving personal property is virtually impossible. Why, then, you might ask, do industry leaders like IBM, Apple Computer, and VisiCorp sell software for personal computers that include "license agreements" that purport to become binding the moment you open the package (see Fig. 8.1)? Let's look at the elements of such an "agreement" for the answer:

It recites rights provided by law

1. You can use the program on a single machine. The "agreement" does not state any *specific* machine, hence the only thing this prohibits is using the program on two or more machines simultaneously. This is a feat that would require you to make copies, which is a prohibited act under the copyright statutes.

2. You can make backup copies. This also is a right provided by the copyright statutes.

Transfer rights

3. You can transfer the program to someone else so long as only the original and backup copies are transferred and only if the copyright notice is maintained. As the saying goes, this is giving "sleeves out of a vest"; the right to sell or transfer personal property cannot be unilaterally abridged and the requirement that the copyright notice be maintained is a matter of law.

Warranty disclaimer

4. The "limited warranty" on the programs is actually a waiver of all warranties. The "agreement" notes, however, that some states (most, in fact) do not allow the waiver of all warranties, and that in those cases state law would apply.

Replace defective goods

5. Defective diskettes or cassettes on which the program is furnished *will* be replaced if they prove defective, or, if they cannot be, you have the right to terminate the "agreement."

Waive all liability

6. All liabilities for ordinary and consequential damages are disclaimed, except where this waiver may be overriden by state law.

7. The "agreement" is governed by the vendor's local law. This is a gratuitous entry as everything included (other than waivers of obligations) is defined by either federal or local state laws.

In summary, "license agreements" in retail transactions are merely notices to the customer

In summary, most retail "license agreements" for software are nothing more than notice to the customer of rights and obligations provided by law *plus* a waiver of any and all obligations or warranties that can be legally avoided.

In some cases these "license agreements" go too far, attempting to restrict usage to a designated machine or imposing conditions of confidentiality, but these are almost certainly unenforceable "wish-I-coulds," thrown in for good measure by the vendor's attorney.

You might wonder why responsible vendors would turn to the device of an ersatz "license agreement" to remind customers of their copyright obligations and to recite waivers of warranty and liability. The same results could have been achieved through simple notice, prominently displayed. The answer probably lies in (1) the psychological value of an "agreement" over a mere notice, and (2) the remote chance that a local court would respect the waivers. For whatever reason, the dubious use of "license agreements" in retail transactions continues.

The important message is that virtually nothing can be done in a retail sale of software to extend rights and obligations already provided by law. For this reason software authors and publishers are well advised to (1) preserve and protect their rights under the copyright statutes, as set out in Chapter 5, and, in certain cases, (2) attempt to forge a post-sale contractual relationship with the customer.

A post-sale relationship can cover follow-on services and products

When would post-sale relationships between the vendor and the retail customer be desirable? Perhaps when direct "hot line" services are provided, when the vendor offers mail-order updates, or in the rare case where source code is offered for a fee. In any of these cases a direct contractual relationship between the parties *can* be forged as the offer can be made to sell follow-on services or products only after prior receipt of a contract, even if the contract is simply a postcard setting forth the terms of the sale.

...Which is generally a good idea

To limit consequential damage claims

In fact, it is a good and recommended practice for vendors who sell their products through independent distribution chains to offer the end user an easy-to-accept offer for post-sale services (e.g., some *real* warranty, however limited, or annual updates). Such an offer could be made in return for a signed agreement that might actually contain an enforceable waiver of implied warranties and liabilities, especially any liability for consequential damages.

Consequential damages are those damages resulting from the use of a faulty product or service (e.g., the loss of a critical file may result in lost sales or profits). The lost profits, in addition to the cost of reconstructing the records, could be awarded as consequential damages if a vendor was held to have breached an express or implied contractual performance obligation. Despite explicit waivers, consequential damages have been awarded under the UCC. A post-sale agreement to limit liability for consequential damages, in return for specific services, has a better chance of being enforceable.

As a follow-on agreement between the parties to a retail transaction should contain similar terms to a true software license, the balance of this chapter will apply, subject only to the caveat that a vendor might have to settle for fewer waivers by the retail purchaser merely to get *any* follow-on agreement (or even the purchaser's name and address).

Ownership

Licenses, unlike outright sales, can contain stringent restrictions on the customer

When you purchase a book or a cassette tape you own it. You are then free to do anything you wish with that property as long as you do not violate the copyright. The same thing applies to software. You can reverse-engineer the product or use its ideas and designs freely. As previously noted, it is difficult or impossible to transfer restrictive covenants in the sale of personal property, so only illegal copying can be proscribed.

This is *not* true, however, when you license someone to use your property; in fact, if no sale takes place the *only* rights the customer gains are those specified in the license agreement. Obviously, in the protection of intangible assets like software, licensing someone to use your property is the preferred transaction.

Typically, only the right to use the software transfers

Your license agreement should make clear that you retain all rights, title, and interest in the underlying property. The "consideration" you are giving, presumably in return for a license fee, should simply be a right to use the property, subject to specified constraints.

Custom development presents special problems

The difference between a sale and a transfer of usage rights may seem obvious, but it is amazing how many contracts fail to specify ownership of the underlying asset or any derivatives made from it. This is especially true in custom-development contracts where the rights in the underlying ideas and designs may be of critical import to both parties.

When both parties have a legitimate ownership interest

Consider the case where a company hires an outside contractor to develop a system that will enable the company to compete more effectively. The contractor is selected based on prior expertise in the field. The resulting system contains many of the ideas and expert knowledge the contractor built up over the years. Could the customer prevent the contractor from using its added experience to develop an even better system for a competitor? Does the customer have all of the rights in and title to the software developed?

In this example you can see the legitimate conflict between the parties: the buyer's interest in protecting what it paid for and the contractor's interest in continuing to use its expertise in subsequent employment. If not specified by contract, a court would have to balance these competing interests, to no one's benefit.

Only a contract can avoid conflicts

The right solution is to have the contract spell everything out. In the example given, it would be usual for the buyer to obtain all of the copyrights in the programs produced at its expense but to have any trade secrets and the right to use same in the production of similar programs remain with the vendor. If you are the vendor, you will probably want the buyer to guarantee to protect those trade secrets, a separate topic to be addressed shortly.

The key point on ownership is that it must be stated explicitly. If the software is to be marketed to more than one buyer, ownership should remain with the vendor.

Transfer of Copyrights

As noted in Chapter 5, the copyright law allows a software buyer to make backup copies but precludes any other copying. The right to produce derivative works remains with the copyright owner. For example, for software used as a component of a larger system, this restriction might run counter to the intent of the transaction and a specific transfer of the right to make derivative works might be required.

You may have to pass some of your copyrights to your customer (e.g., the right to make derivatives)

In general, any permitted copying of your software or any use of your software to make a derivative work should be specified in writing, preferably in standard documentation that can be referenced by the license agreement. Your agreement should say, for example, that you transfer to the customer a limited right to make copies and derivative works, but solely as specified in the documentation provided with the software. It is good practice to remind the customer of the continuing obligation to include your copyright notice in these permitted copies.

Contractual Protection of Confidential Information

Bypassing contractual guarantees, even once, can void subsequent trade secrecy claims

When software that contains trade secrets is offered as a commercial "product," the vendor must walk a tightrope between the desire to reach the widest possible audience and the requirements of trade secrecy. I believe very few vendors have succeeded in this vein and that most would fail a rigorous challenge to their claims of trade secrecy.

The reason is straightforward: Trade secrecy requires an agreement between the parties. It is common practice to waive, defer, or modify commercial agreements in the desire to make a sale. If the nondisclosure provisions are set aside, even once, the vendor will find his or her trade secrecy claims difficult to enforce.

Simply put yourself to the test; imagine your adversary's counsel asking you the following question under oath: "Do you know of *any* situation in which your company or its agents provided the materials in question to a prospect or customer who had not agreed in advance to treat the material as secret?" If your answer is not an unqualified "no," you are both typical and on dangerous ground. If you have gone so far as to routinely distribute "trial" copies of your software without contracts, copyright is your only hope.

Simply labeling every-thing does not create an obligation of trust

One-way agreements do not solve the problem; i.e., you cannot simply label something as confidential and subsequently claim that the recipient had entered into a confidential relationship. As noted in Chapter 6, *implied* agreements can exist, but both parties must be involved. The recipient of a trade secret must know that it is a secret *and* agree to keep it secret; otherwise no basis of trust exists.

But even simple nondisclosure agreements are effective

Even very simple nondisclosure agreements will suffice. It is not necessary for the entire commercial relationship to be put in place; the confidential relationship can be established in one or two sentences. A clever approach is to arm sales representatives with postcard-like agreements that generally will not require a prolonged legal review (if any). These "easy-to-sign" agreements can and should be in plain English (see Fig. 8.2). This simple step will suffice until the actual license agreement is negotiated and signed.

Sir or Madam:
We are negotiating a mutal relationship that will involve proprietary software. To further our discussions you have agreed to disclose trade secrets and other confidential information and we have agreed to keep the information confidential and use it only as you specify. Our signatures indicate our acceptance of these terms.

\---   \---
   [Receiving Party]   [Provider]

\---   \---
     [Date]   [Name of Software]

FIGURE 8.2   SAMPLE "POSTCARD" NONDISCLOSURE AGREEMENT

Elements of a License Agreement

There are eight key items to include in your license agreement to insure the protection of your trade secrets and other confidential information after the sale is complete:

Definitions are important

1. Define the subject matter well. Make sure that the agreement extends to *all* of the materials you will transfer, including confidential training, notes, and documentation, as well as the programs. (See Chapter 2 for a comprehensive definition of "software.")

Nonexclusive and nontransferrable

2. The customer should agree that the license provided is limited to a right to use the software as specified in writing by you, that it is nontransferrable and nonexclusive (i.e., you remain free to license others to use the same software). You may wish to allow transfer of the agreement to a purchaser of substantially all of the customer's assets.

Acknowledge trade secrets

Title stays with you

3. The customer should acknowledge that the software that will be licensed from you contains valuable trade secrets and other proprietary rights, including copyrights, and that all rights, title, and interest in the software shall remain yours except as specifically provided in the agreement.

Usage limited to one machine or location

4. Limit the location(s) in which the software may be used (e.g., to as little as one machine or to a specified address). It is reasonable to grant the user the right to substitute another machine or location but that should be subject to your approval. You may wish to grant the customer a temporary right to transfer the software to a backup machine or location in the event of a loss of the primary site, but this should (1) require notification at the time of transfer, and (2) be for a limited duration without formal approval.

Derivatives are your property

5. The customer should agree that any derivative works (i.e, modifications or enhancements to the software) are included in the subject matter being licensed (i.e., they are your property and are subject to all of the licensing terms).

Agents and employees must be included

Physical security

A standard of care must be established

6. The customer must agree to maintain the confidence of the licensed materials. This should include maintaining your notice of confidentiality and copyright on all copies or derivatives, restricting access to those who have entered into nondisclosure agreements, and providing physical security.

Frequently the customer will have internal procedures for the handling of confidential materials and standard agreements with employees and agents that can be referenced. Regardless of the words used, however, it is critical that a "standard of care" be established and that the customer agrees to at least use its "best efforts" to maintain your licensed materials in confidence.

Exempt nonconfidential items; notice required

The customer may demand, and you should be prepared to give, a waiver on any materials that now or later are generally disclosed and on any materials that are not transferred with confidential notice. Note the burden this places on your day-to-day operations, but note also that *all* of your trade secret rights can be lost by a general disclosure (see Chapter 6).

Damages may be incalculable

7. Require customer agreement that the damages you would suffer as a result of a breach of its confidentiality obligations would extend beyond the scope of the agreement and could be incalculable. Require the right to temporary and permanent injunctive relief in the event of such breach. This is important as only the prevention of further distribution will protect the confidentiality and trade secret status of the material.

Specify termination procedures

8. At the end of the contract term (including any early termination) the customer should be bound to return or certify the destruction of all confidential information. The agreement between the parties should state that the customer's confidentiality obligations shall survive termination.

The foregoing would apply equally to custom-development contracts, with the following exceptions:

Transferring copyrights, not title, can be better for both parties

1. The customer may demand title to the software. If trade secrets are involved this should be avoided. A broader transfer of rights may be required, however, including the right to use the software freely, modify it, and create copies. Generally a transfer of copyrights will suffice (in fact, for taxation purposes, the customer may be better off simply accepting the copyright). The vendor should retain all rights in the trade secrets employed, but may have to agree to a noncompete provision in return. If this is required, a narrowly drawn agreement, preferably naming no more than a handful of proscribed future customers or a very narrow sub-industry, is strongly recommended.

Consider competition

2. The restrictions on customer use will normally be more liberal, e.g., the customer may have the right to freely transfer the software and to use it to create derivative works. If this is the case, be sure to spell out the limits applicable to transfers. For example, could the customer license copies to others? If not restricted, you may wish to include a royalty agreement and assurances

that the customer's clients will honor your rights in the trade secrets.

License Agreements: Remedies

Require agreements with the customer's agents and employees

A disclosure of your trade secrets, even if it is inadvertent, can forever place them in the public domain. If a customer's employee or agent makes such a disclosure, the customer should be held responsible. If, for example, a group of your customer's employees left to form a business that used trade secrets (e.g., software) provided by you under license to their former employer, you *might* be able to proceed against them directly under the local state's trade secrecy laws, but you would have to demonstrate that a confidential relationship existed. (Note that no such relationship is necessary to proceed on a copyright violation, which is a good reason to protect your copyrights, as noted in Chapter 5). This is the most important protection provided by commercial software licenses. It is not a breach of trust by the licensee that should be feared most; your contract will protect you adequately. Rather, it is a breach by someone who benefits indirectly from your customer's access to the trade secrets, especially the customer's agents and employees.

. . . So the customer will be responsible, even if the third party claims to be an "innocent infringer"

By insisting that disclosures of your trade secrets to agents and employees of your customer be made only after a confidential relationship has been established, you eliminate the possibility of a third party acquiring the information innocently, which leaves you with no recourse. If your customer has not applied an appropriate standard of care in handling the material, your contract will have been breached; if an appropriate standard of care was employed, you can easily demonstrate that the third party did not get your trade secrets innocently.

If the links are all in place, i.e., between you and the customer and between the customer and its agents and employees, your chances to negotiate a fair resolution of any trade secrecy or unfair competition threats are substantial. The key is the customer's liability for any "downstream" disclosures; this insures that the full economic, marketplace, and negotiating muscle of the customer will be on your side if a problem arises.

Other Considerations

Obviously, there are many other considerations in drafting software license agreements. While the scope of this book is limited to the protection of software, you will also want to address these additional topics in your agreements:

1. Access to enhancements and updates.
2. Warranties or waivers of same, especially any obligations to repair program defects. Whatever your terms, it is important to avoid applicability of the Uniform Commercial Code, however unlikely, with a prominent statement that the terms of the warranty are in lieu of any others, express or implied, including warranties of merchantability and fitness for a specific purpose.
3. Installation and training obligations.
4. Terms of agreement and renewal options, if any.
5. Payment terms and penalties for late payments.
6. Restrictions on data center or service bureau usage, if any.
7. Customer obligations to provide personnel, computer facilities, etc.
8. Trial period and return conditions, if any.
9. Infringement of patents and copyrights. The customer will generally request indemnification, and it is a reasonable and low-risk undertaking to offer it as a standard contract clause.
10. Limitations on the customer's rights to modify the software; warranty implications.
11. Liability limitations. This is *very* important, especially in waivers of liability for consequential damages. You cannot, however, prevent liability in the case of fraud or tort, so you might as well agree to same.
12. Default conditions, opportunities to remedy defects, and termination conditions.
13. General terms. Governing law, arbitration provisions (generally undesirable), *force majeure* waivers, severability (i.e., a holding that any part of the agreement is invalid would not invalidate the whole agreement).

Manage your attorney

As a general rule, data processing agreements tend to be overburdened with legal language, possibly because the subject matter is foreign to the lawyer who drafted them. To avoid constant bickering with prospects, try writing in simple language the agreement you would *like* to have before you give it to a lawyer. Take the customer's point of view and give reasonable guarantees in advance. Put the strength where you need it (i.e., in protecting your proprietary rights and limiting your liabilities). Tell your attorney that he or she can re-write but not expand (i.e., that your five-page agreement must stay five pages, and that middle-English is unacceptable). Hold your ground.

9 NAMING YOUR SOFTWARE

Introduction

Your good name has value

Although not strictly an issue of software protection, the name you give your software may have significant commercial value that you will want to protect. As software has moved into the mass marketplace, trade names for some of the better known products have gained wide commercial recognition and hence value. Buyers will pay more for a well-known brand name and may even use a brand name to describe a generic product they wish to buy. It is in this light that protecting the name you give your software, along with the software itself, takes on added importance.

Names are protected by state and federal laws

Trademarks exist under state-by-state common laws and under federal statutes. The overall intent of both the common laws and the statutes is to prevent the unfair competition that could arise if two identifying names were sufficiently close to confuse a buyer. In general, assuming the two trade names were sufficiently similar and the products were being sold to a common audience, the first to use the name would have rights to the name.

Establishing Rights to a Trademark

Under state law, market definition is important

Simply using a trademark gives you common-law rights to continue its use, presuming you were the first to do so. This is generally true for markets that do not overlap, but two identical names would not be found to infringe each other if they were used in distinctly different markets. A product sold in the Northeast, for example, would not be found to infringe the trademark of a product sold exclusively in the South, despite the similarity of names and markets.

Federal registration brings major benefits

This is not the case if the trademark is registered with the Patent and Trademark Office (PTO). Federal registration gives the holder the rights to the trademark anywhere the business is conducted, now or in the future. Local use of a confusingly similar name is not a defense against a federally registered trademark. Because the rights are conveyed by federal law (the Lanham Act of 1946), suit may be brought in federal court, which is a major advantage for out-of-state plaintiffs. Federal registration also can be used to enjoin the use of the same trademark on foreign products that are sold domestically.

Federal registration will not, however, automatically squelch uses of the trademark that predated your registration. For a period of five years, your registration can be contested by anyone who can demonstrate prior use. Even after your trademark becomes "incontestable," which occurs when you file a declaration of continued use after five years, you may not be able to prevent a similar name from being used if its use predated yours. However, the converse is that your trademark cannot be suppressed by an earlier user.

Registering Your Trademark

What you *cannot* register

You cannot register names that:

are generic or merely descriptive (e.g., "word processor")

the PTO considers immoral, scandalous, or otherwise unfit

include proper names (e.g., your name or your town's name) unless these are already well established as a trademark

would be confused with another name, even if not identical, if the other name is for similar goods or services.

Do a preregistration search

The last item can be avoided by a preregistration search of both existing registered trademarks and other names in common use that might block your registration. These searches are now done by commercial search firms who use computerized search routines to provide a raw list at $100 to $150 per name. Expect your attorney to mark up this fee, however, as these search services are generally unavailable to individuals. Recently, however, on-line trademark searches have been made available to personal computer users via Lockheed's Dialog service. It is obviously a good idea to do a search before you launch a new product: The money you spend promoting the name could otherwise be wasted.

How to proceed

Assuming your trademark passes the preceding hurdles, federal registration requires the filing of some forms, five identical specimens of the trademark's use, and a $35 fee. Forms and instructions are available from the Patent and Trademark Office, Washington, D.C. 20231. Legal assistance from a patent and trademark attorney is advised, not only because of the filing burdens involved but also because there can be several follow-up steps, including arguing your case should the PTO reject your trademark as being too similar to another, which is a frequent occurrence.

Foreign regulations vary

Your trademark can also be registered in foreign markets, but each country approaches the issue differently. In some countries, no common-law trademark exists. In some, the trademark must be in use for a specified number of years before it is eligible for registration. In many countries, *any* name containing descriptive components will be rejected. (I had the trademark "KEY/MASTER" rejected because a "key" and a "master" were the names of things!)

Notice and Infringement

Giving notice is easy

Once you have chosen your trademark, denote the fact that it is a trademark by using either the characters "TM" or an "R" in a circle. The letters "TM" should be used for trademarks protected by common law or for names in the process of federal registration. The "R" in a circle is used for trademarks that have been registered. Both should appear in the upper right-hand corner of the name at its first appearance in every published work and on all labels. For example:

WIDGET™

Policing use is important

Whether it is registered or not, it is important to protect your trademark by defending it rigorously. This means policing trade journals and the like for the use of your trademark by others, and then demanding that such use is ceased immediately. If the use is legitimate (i.e., a reference to your products or services), you must insist that the user state that the trademark is your property.

**Beware the
generic name**

Trademarks can be lost if they become generic. This has happened with such widely known names as aspirin and cellophane. No one in the software business has been successful enough to have a trademark endangered as generic, but it will happen soon. When it does, it probably will have been helped along if the owner of the trademark used the mark generically. You can avoid this by *never* using your trademark in a descriptive way and by never permitting anyone else to do so either. Other industries have learned this trick; simply say, "Our Widget brand word processor is . . ." rather than "Our Widget is . . . ."

A Few Other Comments

**Twenty plus
twenty plus . . .**

Your federally registered trademark gives you statutory rights for twenty years. As long as the trademark is still in commercial use you can renew this for successive twenty-year periods. You will lose the trademark if you fail to renew it, fail to make the mandatory declaration of its continued use between the fifth and sixth year after registration, or have the registration successfully contested during this five-year period.

**You must use
the mark in
interstate commerce**

Federal registration applies only to goods used in interstate commerce, but this should include virtually all software. Even if you are operating only locally you can establish interstate use by a single shipment out of your home state. It is good practice, in fact, if you intend to operate on an interstate basis to make *any* shipment as early as possible to satisfy the registration requirement.

In closing, I advise that you pay closer attention to your product names. Make sure they are federally registered and establish a formal program for monitoring the use of infringing names. (One good way to do this is simply to send a memo to your employees asking them to clip out and forward any articles or ads that contain similar product names.) Examine all your ads and published documents to be sure the registration notice is where it should be. Also, be sure to enforce your rights to your trademarks vigorously or you will lose them.

10 PHYSICAL BARRIERS TO THEFT

Introduction: The Usefulness of Mechanical Protection Schemes

Nothing will stop a determined thief. However, this does not mean that mechanical means of preventing theft should be dismissed as useless. Rather, physical barriers should be used to make theft less attractive, as part of a larger program.

Five classes of thief

There are five classes of software thief:

1. The individual who makes a copy of someone else's program

2. The dealer or distributor who "throws in" a "free" copy of some software in order to sell hardware

3. The competitor, ex-employee, or agent who uses an illicit copy of the software to develop a competing derivative product

4. The noncommercial, but organized, "shadow" distribution networks (usually computer clubs but more and more frequently

including corporations distributing copies of software to their employees)

5. The serious "pirate" who mass-reproduces and markets unauthorized copies of a legitimate product.

Despite publicity, the hacker isn't the big threat

There is no denying the problem the first two categories represent, but the attention of the press (and of too many software vendors) has overemphasized their importance. The individual thief may not steal a copy of your program if you make the barriers tough enough, but he or she probably will not buy a copy either. After obtaining an illicit copy, the "hacker" will more than likely move on, the thrill being in the chase. In other cases, where the thief is also a legitimate prospect, the initial copy made may be an unauthorized "demo," which frequently leads to a delayed sale.

"I just borrowed it to try it out"

The problem of individual thievery is a real one for certain classes of products, but not all. Very few individuals are going to be willing to rely for long on illicit and unsupported copies of system, database management, or important application software (e.g., to prepare their income taxes). These same users are, however, very likely to "borrow" a copy of such software to see if the price is justified. If physical barriers make it easier to try out and buy a competitive package, the vendor has potentially done more harm than good. For high-priced software, other incentives to become a legitimate user are often superior to physical barriers (e.g., follow-on services, product updates, etc.).

Games are special

Game software for personal computers is a special class of product that, according to sketchy statistics, is regularly stolen by individuals. Because the game generally has a limited life (i.e., interest in it wanes with time), needs minimal documentation, is typically not updated by the vendor, and requires little or no support, there are few barriers to outright theft and few incentives for a thief to subsequently buy a legitimate copy. This is a class of product that *does* lend itself to physical protections.

Dealers and distributors who want to steal can

But they can be caught, too

Neither the dealer or distributor who fails to pay royalties on software nor the serious commercial "pirate" is going to be easily stopped by physical barriers. If the economic incentives are significant enough, any system can be broken. A better method to stop an errant agent or illegal distributor is to detect illegitimate copies by administrative means (e.g., by matching warranty registration cards, service calls, and upgrade orders against distributor sales records). Legal means, civil and criminal, should then be used to stop the piracy for good.

Clubs are vulnerable

Clubs that distribute multiple copies of software for personal computers generally have the talent available to "crack" any physical protection scheme, but they are also *very* vulnerable to legal action. With almost minimal effort, an individual vendor or a trade association could do sufficient undercover work (e.g., by infiltrating the more significant clubs) to obtain "smoking gun" evidence of copyright violations. That this is not being routinely done suggests that the problem is too small to warrant such action.

Corporations aren't likely to take huge risks

Corporate thievery is generally carried out by an administrative department that appears to be a single customer, but in fact, is a source of redistribution and central support for other users within the organization. Unlike the computer club, a corporation bent on theft is hard to detect. Physical protection schemes can be effective against such practices, but only as one means of raising the cost of illegitimate use. Other means, especially the threat of corporate embarrassment and criminal penalties for responsible executives, are more likely to succeed. A vendor subject to such theft should certainly put an educational program and other means of controlling internal redistribution (e.g., corporate licenses) ahead of physical barriers.

Agents and employees know their way around (barriers)

The ex-employee or agent who sets up shop to compete is generally going to start with source programs or other unprotected copies of the software. In most cases, the software is not even easily identifiable as a pilfered copy; this must be established by indirect means (i.e., "striking similarities" that could not have been accidental, unreasonably short development times, etc.). In any event, physical protection mechanisms apply to this threat only to the extent that they assist in keeping trade secrets and other sensitive information from prying eyes that otherwise would not have access to it.

Use physical means to raise the stakes

In summary, physical barriers are of very limited use in most prospective cases of software misappropriation. If used properly they *can* raise the stakes. For only one class of software product (i.e., cheap mass-produced programs that require little or no ancillary services) are they indispensable.

Physical Protections: An Overview

Physical protections break neatly into two classes: software-based and hardware-based mechanisms. Software-based mechanisms include hidden locks that require external keys, barriers against copying, and encryption. Hardware-based mechanisms include external devices required by the software and alternative delivery means that involve special equipment.

Hardware: Harder to build and harder to beat

In general, hardware-based protection mechanisms are harder and more costly to defeat. Recording the entire program, for example, in ROM (read-only memory) and distributing it as a hardware addition to the computer system will defeat all but the professional thief with hardware manufacturing resources. This extreme level of protection will also prevent the vendor from providing low-cost updates and maintenance.

Hardware + software = software

Combining hardware-based and software-based mechanisms solves this problem, but also lowers the barriers to a potential thief. Requiring a special piece of hardware that the software must identify before it will execute means that the verification routine in the program could be identified and crippled by a clever technician; no production facilities are required.

Software is easy to beat

The most common forms of physical protection mechanism are solely software-based. In general, such routines rely on programmed barriers against copying or embedded routines that require external information before "unlocking" the software for use. If these mechanisms are static, they are also easy for a determined thief to defeat as, once again, the mechanism can be identified and crippled by a software modification. Certain encryption schemes can make life more difficult for the thief, but, in the final analysis, if the mechanism appears in a "dump" of the program, no matter how cleverly it is hidden, a competent technician can disarm it.

Hardware Protection Mechanisms

Manufacturers of game software for personal computers have already learned that there is *nothing,* other than distributing the game on special hardware, that will prevent significant levels of unauthorized distribution. Game software distributed on "floppy" disks is widely reported to have four illegal copies in circulation for every legitimate one. Copy protection schemes for floppy disks all rely on easily broken techniques, and an entire industry has grown up selling programs to copy "uncopyable" programs.

The newer personal computers help . . .

Newer computer systems for home use do not rely solely on floppy disks for program input, and this trend will continue. IBM's PC-Jr., for example, combines the features of a general-purpose personal computer with cartridge-loaded software that was previously found only on special-purpose game machines. While the stakes are higher for the independent software developer who wants to reach this market, they become incredibly high for all but the organized thief.

. . . As cartridges are harder to copy

Software cartridges generally rely on ROM as the recording medium for the programs, which means that specialized facilities are required to produce (or duplicate) the product. Even so, hardware routines are already on the market that will "trap" and save a program as it is running in the main memory of a computer. This means that a ROM-based program could be redistributed on a low-cost floppy disk *if* (and this is key) the ROM was not repetitively accessed during the program's execution.

The hardware must be essential

The critical determinant of the success of any hardware-based protection scheme is the degree to which the hardware element is essential to the operation of the software. ROM containing large program overlays, for example, which are dynamically fetched as needed into the computer's main memory, will not be easily replaced or duplicated. Conversely, a currently popular scheme involving a hardware "chip" that the software accesses merely for identification purposes will only be a barrier to the casual thief and is frequently a real burden for the legitimate user.

Software Protections

Three approaches

Programmed protection mechanisms fall into three classes: barriers to copying, encryption, and access locks. Barriers to copying generally are used only with microcomputer software that is mass-distributed on floppy disks. While encryption is increasingly popular as a means of protecting information that is in transit (e.g., across telephone lines), its use for software protection has generally been limited to securing the trade secrecy status of confidential materials. Access locks have been used primarily for licensed software subject to usage restrictions (e.g., a specific machine, term of use, etc.).

For personal computers, copy-protect schemes are still king

Making distribution disks copy-resistant is currently the most popular form of protection for mass-merchandized software. The schemes used are based on varying the format of the data (i.e., programs) recorded on the disk so as to render them uncopyable by standard software. Obviously, since anything written to a disk by mechanical means can later be read back, someone wishing to make a copy need only discover the format of the "uncopyable disk." The most popular methods of varying the format involve (1) recording on otherwise empty areas of the disk, or (2) using areas of the disk that normally contain timing and other control information for codes or program storage.

A brief introduction to disk protection

Recording disks are divided into a series of concentric circles called *tracks*. The data on each track is preceded and/or followed by special characters that are used on read-back to identify the data portion and thus compensate for different speeds of rotation. For standard disks, to avoid interference when each track is written or read, a number of physical tracks (i.e., tracks on which the recording mecha-

**The disk appears
to be abnormal**

nism *could* be positioned) are left blank between each track with actual data.

Because the reading of data from a floppy disk drive is generally under program control, the system software to read the disk must either be loaded from the disk itself or be resident in the computer's permanent storage. In most cases, this software is loaded from a special section of the disk and is then given control to read the rest of the disk. Most disk protection schemes capitalize on this by recording data on the disk in normally unused areas (e.g., in the area of each track normally used for synchronization characters or by varying the normal spacing between tracks). The program to control the disk read-write mechanism is recorded in a standard place and format, but it "knows" its own data format and thus can get the programs off the disk and into main memory to run. Other programs, of course, would expect a normally formatted disk and fail at the copying effort.

**But this hurts the
legitimate user, too**

This form of copy protection is cheap and reasonably effective against the casual thief. Unfortunately, it also means that the legitimate user cannot make the backup copies he or she is legally entitled to make. Some vendors have tried to get around the backup problem by including a special routine on their copy-protected disk that will make an "inactive" backup copy, i.e., one that will not run until "activated." Activating the backup copy requires deactivating the primary copy, usually by a small routine that reads and cripples a small area of the primary copy, then unlocks an equivalent in the backup (which now becomes the master). The advantage of this scheme is that it allows an endless chain of backup copies to be made. The disadvantage is obvious—enough of the master must be readable to activate the backup copy. In cases of theft, loss, or complete destruction, the user is out of luck.

**...And are
easily beaten**

The determined thief can, of course, locate the small invariant program that controls the reading of the disk and discover the copy-protected disk's special format. Alternatively, since this program is usually on the distribution disk, a "copy anything" routine, which reproduces data regardless of format, can make illegal copies that remain individually protected against standard copying.

Encryption: Its Limited Use

Encryption is the rendering of a data or information stream unintelligible except through use of an decryption algorithm that precisely reverses the process. Encryption goes back thousands of years as a means of encoding messages. In times of war, deciphering the enemy's code books can mean more than any weapon.

Unfortunately, despite dramatic advances in the science of encryption, these techniques apply more to insuring privileged communications than they do to software protection. The reason is simple: If you can get hold of the decoded message, why fool around trying to break the code? In computer systems as we know them today, the program that the computer executes must be object code, unadorned and unadulterated. The published specifications for the object code of the computer system are there for anyone who needs or wants them.

All a software pirate need do is avoid the encryptified distribution and concentrate on the decryptified object program. If the secrets in the software are the goal, decompilers and reverse assemblers help this process by converting the relatively obscure object code back into something more easily understood. More typically, however, simply capturing the object code in a running machine will allow the program to be transferred to (and run on) another identical machine.

Access Locks

Back in the early 1960s, when the software industry was in its infancy, a colleague thought he had the perfect protection scheme. His program, a library maintenance routine for source programs, was programmed to cease operations if the date and serial number of the computer being used did not match the legitimate "keys" provided with each copy. (On the medium-scale IBM equipment for which his program was designed, the date and serial number are accessible under program control.) Unfortunately, his programmers forgot about leap years, and February 29, 1968 became a date few of his customers will ever forget. On that date, which was "illegal" to the security mechanism, every single copy of the program ceased operation.

As with other forms of protection, access locks must be used with extreme care so legitimate users are not hurt or disuaded from using the software. This approach tends to apply best in circumstances where the software is licensed for a limited period of time or for a specific group of machines, which in general means that access keys apply to larger machines and more expensive software.

In larger computer installations, running with the right date is generally essential. Payroll and other accounting routines, date stamps on revisions, etc., all rely on the internal clock for the time and date. In smaller machines this is not as true. Also, many smaller machines do not provide programmed access to the machine's serial number. Lastly, because of the complexity (and dangers) of this approach, a one-on-one relationship between the vendor and the customer is essential, ruling out access locks for software sold or licensed through independent third parties.

Control who, when, and on what

Access locks are simply programmed checks that the software is being used on the right machine within the authorized license period and by the right customer. These variables are typically supplied to the program by a coded message each time the program is run. A "hidden" routine in the software then compares the current expiration date for the user's license with today's date, the machine serial number with an authorized machine list, and the password identifying the customer with the owner of the license. Because the message that unlocks the software could be transferred with an illegal copy, the message must be changed frequently, and the new "keys" must be tightly controlled.

Hidden transients

The machine-readable keys are usually encryptified, although a new password must obviously be disclosed to the licensee so the machine operator can initiate the program. The decryptification and verification routine is usually a well-hidden transient program (i.e., something that is called into main memory, executed, then overlaid with another routine) that would not appear in an ordinary storage "dump."

The same old problem

Obviously, access keys share a common disadvantage with all software barriers: They are easily defeated by any competent programmer. No matter how well hidden the testing routine is, a computer is a logical beast that does only what it is told; this means that, with patience, the secrets of even the most complex program can be unlocked. Furthermore, the close relationship required between the software vendor and the customer makes other means of protecting the software, (e.g., contractual guarantees) all that more attractive.

Conclusion

Unless you have a real problem, it would be better to use other approaches

Most readers are going to find the conclusion I reach on mechanical protection mechanisms an unhappy one. Nonetheless, it appears obvious that these schemes are useful *only* as a means of protecting the casual thief and may hinder the legitimate user. Unless casual thievery is a *real* problem for the software you market, the economic value

Optical disks may add an option

of complex physical security is limited at best. If casual thievery *is* a problem of magnitude, you can raise the barriers by using the methods described, but that is all you can hope for.

Read-only distribution devices (now primarily ROM cartridges) provide the ultimate barrier against the individual thief, but they will not deter the professional pirate. More read-only devices will be available to the software marketer in the near future, especially optical disks. Whether they can be widely used for program protection remains an open question. Their very existence will create more demands for legitimate copying, just as the availability of "hard Winchester" storage devices created huge customer demand for mechanisms to put legitimate copies of protected programs onto these newer mass-storage devices. Whatever the answer, it is certain that mechanical protections will merely supplement other means of software protection, most importantly economic and legal incentives to behave honestly.

11

PUBLIC POLICY AND THE FUTURE OF SOFTWARE PROTECTION

Introduction

You can influence change

The focus of this book has thus far been on what a prudent business-man should know and do *today,* given the current status of our laws and technologies. There is change in the wind, however, and anyone with a genuine interest in the subject of software protection is in a position to influence that change.

Through trade associations, court cases, and just doing business

How? Most of the major data processing trade associations have already taken or will soon take formal positions on a wide range of legislative recommendations. In court case after court case, pioneering companies and individuals are helping to shape the interpretation of existing laws to modern circumstances. Many businessmen are dramatically involved in the growing conflict between the U.S. Department of Commerce (con) and the rest of the Administration (pro) on the use of software export licenses as a means to stem the flow of "critical technology" to potential adversaries.

127

For whatever reason, it is hard be involved in the business of software production or distribution without being forced to develop opinions and positions on a variety of unsettled issues.

The purpose of the discussion that follows will be to focus on the issues before our legislators, courts, and public officials that involve public policy on software. In the process, some of the risks inherent in following the recommendations of the preceding ten chapters, which have attempted to sink a foundation in shifting sands, should be manifest.

The Overriding Legislative Issue

The overriding issue: can the existing system work?

There is basically one overriding question concerning the legal protection of software: Can software be adequately protected within our existing legal framework? The answer (and the debate itself) raises a sub-issue: What are the specific legislative changes necessary to either supplement or replace the existing system?

Evolution generally being preferable to revolution, the greatest effort today is being expended on modifying our laws to meet the anticipated long-term needs of software producers, vendors, and users. The following changes or proposed additions to existing statutes illustrate the key issues under debate:

Patent law changes

1. Revise the patent laws to eliminate the ambiguities produced by a series of vague and contradictory court cases. Specifically, make the patentability of software (which meets other traditional tests) a statutory right.

Copyright revisions

2. Modify the copyright laws to eliminate confusions produced in the wording of the existing legislation. Specifically:
   a. Broaden the statute's existing definition of a "program" in order to insure that *all* of the various forms a program can take, from its detailed block diagram through its implementation in firmware, are protected.
   b. Make even clearer Congress's intent that trade secrecy and copyright can coexist in the same work.
   c. Legitimatize (in the U.S.) a machine-processable copyright notice (e.g., (c)).
   d. Mandate a system of secure deposit (or waiver of deposit) for works that contain confidential information.
   e. Implement equivalent changes in the Universal Copyright Convention in order to insure international acceptance of copyright protections for software.

New "design" legislation

3. Implement so-called "design legislation" to provide unique protections, beyond those (theoretically) available through the patent and copyright systems, to otherwise unprotectable designs, processes, and ideas.

Stronger penalties

4. Pass "piracy legislation" to create or strengthen penalties that can be imposed on software thieves.

Federal trade secrecy

5. Implement a Federal Trade Secrecy Act to replace the state-by-state protections now available.

But, if new legislation *is* needed . . .

There are those who argue, however, that software *cannot* be adequately protected under existing legal systems, even with careful revision. Assuming this position has validity, a question remains as to what type of "sui generis" (i.e., unique) legislation should be enacted.

Is the "software is unique" view right?

1. Should it follow the Model Provisions of the Protection of Computer Software proposed by the World Intellectual Property Organization (WIPO),[76] whose proposals marry a copyright-like notice and deposit system with patent-like protections on designs and ideas?

Or do we need broader revisions?

2. Alternatively, is our entire system of protecting the rights of authors and inventors out of tune with modern technology, in which case should we consider a complete rewrite of these laws, not just for software, but for all intellectual property?

A Philosophical Position Must Precede Debate on the Issues

A question of public policy

It is impossible to address these specific questions without first examining the philosophy behind the constitutional mandate that the works of inventors and authors be protected. This is not an academic question; there is a genuine question of public policy here. How do you balance the need for economic incentives on creativity with the general public's need for information and lowest-priced goods?

Balance is needed

Our founding fathers clearly could not anticipate electronic publishing, broadcasting, software, or a world linked by satellites. The claim by many Third World countries that existing patent and copyright laws slow their development and promote a form of economic colonialism might have found a sympathetic audience in our own colonial time. And yet, the rampant theft of those same satellite signals, "knock offs" of patented products flowing in across national borders to compete with legitimate goods, and widespread illegal copying have clearly caused economic harm for the producers. Such damage must eventually result in fewer innovative goods and services for the consumer.

How long should an inventor enjoy a monopoly?

Where should the balance be? Is it reasonable to give someone a monopoly on an invention for seventeen years? Why not five or fifty? And what is an "invention"? Is it reasonable to say that biological engineering can produce "inventions" but that mathematical equations expressing heretofore unknown concepts merely define "laws of nature"?

What creative activity deserves protection?

The trick is to avoid the "angels on pinhead" syndrome. The real question is: What creative activities should have statutory protections against independent invention and copying, and for how long?

Should independent invention be penalized?

The threat of independent invention is the most interesting to discuss. Why *ever* preclude someone from profiting from an independent invention? The argument is that the inventor needs a fixed period in which a monopoly will insure that the costs of research can be recouped and a reasonable profit can be earned. This protection, it is argued, stimulates investment and risk-taking. But what about the inventor who spent just as much on the same invention but finished second? How is the public interest best served? Clearly *not* by statutory protections that discourage independent invention or provide long-term monopolies; the wave of technology is simply rolling too fast.

What is a copy?

Another important issue is copying. Is it reasonable to preclude copying of something expressing an idea or a design but allow the idea or design itself to be copied? Why, for example, should it be a precluded act to copy the design documents an architect produced for a building but not the building itself? It is the act of *copying* that causes the harm, not the way the copying took place.

What protections do you *really* want and need?

What do you really want in software protection? Do you want a legislated monopoly? Answer carefully, remembering that your competitor would also enjoy a monopoly. "Just on my *real* inventions," might be your reply, but if your competitor invented it, should that prevent you from independently inventing the same thing? If you are in the business of developing accounting software you certainly would not want a system that gave the first person to develop an accounts receivable package a monopoly (unless, of course, that person was you, and then there's accounts payable, payroll, etc., to think about).

Protection of true inventions; prevention of harmful

In the best of all possible worlds you would probably would want a system that gave you a long-term financial stake in any *real* inventions you made, but that did not let anyone have a monopoly on commonplace advances in technology. You would not want anyone to be able to copy your work in part or in whole, but you probably would be adamant in defending your own right to react to a successful product in the marketplace by building something that did the same job better, even to the point of "reverse engineering" the competing product. You would probably want laws to make sure you are not taken advantage of, especially by ex-employees, agents, and competitors who misappropriate your property.

What existing laws do...

Do the existing laws provide this protection or do we need something new? The intellectual property laws of the industrialized world currently try to protect three entirely different things: invention, unique expression, and commercial expertise. In most countries, as in the United States, patent law applies to the first, copyright to the second, and trade secrecy to the third. Unlike most of the world, the United States does not have a national trade secrecy law, but the high degree of uniformity in state trade secrecy law almost moots the distinction.

...And why they don't do it well

The problem in applying these three forms of protection to something new is not a failure of the underlying concepts but rather the degree to which the statutes and case law have evolved and the problem of "pigeon-holing" something new into an existing format. As a law ages, it acquires appendages and exceptions that reflect special interests or attempts by the legislature to clarify its original intent in the face of errant court interpretations. The U.S. Copyright law is a perfect example of originally sound legislation that has mutated into a hodgepodge of special rules. The fundamental concept of protecting a creative form of expression, however, remains sound.

Can the need be restated?

Is it possible to reexpress the protection needs of modern technology more simply? Perhaps a fresh view would help.

Three levels of creativity

1. For discussion purposes, we should scrap the current legal grouping of works by category (e.g., Is it an industrial good? Is it a writing? etc.). I propose that it would be preferable to segment the creative process and provide specific protections for each step, for example:
   a. invention or discovery of basic principles
   b. development of a unique, novel, and nonobvious process, system, or device
   c. production of something having commercial or artistic value.

Discovery of natural laws,

2. It is probably wrong and unworkable to attempt to provide any restrictions on the first category (the invention or discovery of basic principles). This is not a novel idea as even our most rigorous existing protection scheme, patents, does not today extend to a law of nature.

Unique invention and development,

3. There is a reasonable consensus that unique and nonobvious designs, processes, and systems *should* have special protections, at least until the inventor can recover the cost of the invention and earn a reasonable profit. The validity of such a concept is that, in return for complete disclosure, the inventor should receive protection from competing inventions, but only for a short period. The length of this protection might reasonably depend on the invention (i.e., it may be reasonable to give longer protection to items requiring longer recovery periods, such as drugs, where other federal regulations interfere with natural market conditions).

Production and reproduction

4. There is a broad consensus that copying anything should be illegal if the copying can be shown to cause economic harm. The normal test is access to the copied work, a similarity in the copy that could not possibly have occurred by chance, and clear economic damage. The is no special reason to place a time limit on this restriction.

Competitive advantage

5. Most would agree that confidential information used in a trade or business to gain competitive advantage should be protected against theft and willful disclosure, just as other business assets are protected against theft or willful destruction.

Assuming these overriding principles are acceptable, does unique legislation have to be enacted to accomplish the goals or can the existing system be made to work? More specifically, is the case of software unique?

Special Treatment for Software?

Unique treatment of software

To avoid analogies with other works, errant court decisions, ambiguities in the law, and so on, it has been very tempting to claim that software is a unique work of humans, unlike any other product or service from times past. A claim of uniqueness lends itself to a plea for specialized laws that supercede or replace the more general concepts of trade secrecy, copyright, and patentability.

. . . For unique reasons

These calls for unique treatment of software have arisen in the past from four disparate sources: (1) those who have been rebuffed in attempts to use existing mechanisms, e.g., patents; (2) those who have a special ax to grind, e.g., because a unique definition might allow them to escape local taxation; (3) those academic or institutional "think tanks" that can afford to take a view unrelated to practical politics; and (4) those who truly believe that software is unique.

. . . All wrong.

The problem with this approach is that the very claim of uniqueness can abrogate claims to more conventional protections. In addition, the political practicality of developing a single but specialized view of software throughout the world should throw fear into all but its most naive advocates. Nonetheless, if a strong *logical* case could be made that software is truly unique, this approach might have an outside chance of success. However, as discussed in Chapter 2, software is only unique to the extent that it uses new languages and distribution media, and this has never been a sufficient argument for special treatment of graphic arts, recordings, films, books, or other works that combine tangible and intangible elements.

Basically, software is not unique

The problems facing the software industry are identical to those of other industries and, in all probability, the differences between software distribution and the distribution of films or books will continue to diminish. In the field of packaged courseware, for example, many vendors have already begun to merge the textual and visual portions of their courses with the programs that do the training or test the student. What once was a book and/or film is now digitized information and animation sequences that are indistinguishable from the program that drive them.

. . . And efforts to treat it as such will fail

It is my opinion that efforts to write special software protection laws will fail and, in failing, will weaken attempts to make existing generic legislation stronger. This is not to say that the work of WIPO and others to draft unique legislation has not been useful. To the contrary, such efforts have focused the debate and have highlighted deficiencies in our existing laws. Nonetheless, it would now be better for all concerned if the producers and vendors of all forms of intangible expression were to recognize their common heritage and needs, and demand modern application of ancient principles to protect their property.

Software can be protected by strengthening existing concepts

The basic list of objectives we set forth earlier in this chapter can be achieved within the existing legal framework. No, the patent laws have not yet been applied successfully to software, but it would not take a lot of political effort to get Congress to reaffirm its 1952 view that patents should apply to *all* inventions. Similarly, the copyright law is vague as to what constitutes "fair use," leaves it to a court's judgment to decide what is a "copy," and treats each new form of authorship (literature, films, etc.) as a special case. Conversely, copyright *does* provide the kind of protections most authors want, including criminal penalties. Trade secret laws work well to protect valuable "know how," but they need standardization at the national (or international) level and should better dovetail with patent and copyright protections.

I doubt if there would be many calls for more extensive protections if the existing mechanisms were made to work properly. Many of the special interest requests for new legislation (e.g., for "chip protection," against movie and record piracy, etc.) would vanish if the current provisions of the copyright law were clarified, especially the criminal sanctions and the definition of a "copy."

The True Problem and a Possible Solution

Our technology has outrun our legal system

Before exploring the major proposals that have been made to change or add to our existing laws, it is worth noting that the true problem may not involve software per se; *all* of our new technologies may have outgrown our existing copyright, patent, and trade secret laws. As software is simply another form of intellectual property which, like so many other intangibles, can be a component of a tangible commercial product, the problems of protecting software are identical to the problems faced by all products with a high level of intangible "value added."

It will get worse...

The problem is destined to get worse as the intangible content of our industrial products increases, and it will increase. Is it reasonable to treat software, motion pictures, courseware, recorded music, proprietary databases, patterns (e.g., chip masks), and electronically recorded text as separate entities? A single videodisk, for example, could contain all of these. It could be used as a component in a training system, a machine tool, a game, or as part of a public performance.

...It's a generic problem

The protection issues are generic, not specific: protection of trade secrets, prevention of unauthorized copying and distribution, and an opportunity to be rewarded fairly for true inventions.

With a generic solution

Earlier in this chapter it was noted that two levels of protection should suffice for all forms of intellectual property, namely (1) a short-term monopoly on ideas, designs, and processes that are truly unique, novel, and nonobvious; and (2) an absolute ban on copying another's work for commercial gain. How does this differ from the protection requirements of industrial property in general? Weren't these the original goals of our patent and copyright legislation?

A coordinated rewrite

It may be time to rewrite these laws, not as a software-driven need but for the broader issues mentioned. Perhaps it is also time to enact a federal trade-secrecy statute. Doing everything at once would insure that all of the protections available are interrelated and not contradictory. Nothing dramatic would have to be done to accomplish this task; a national commission could make sense out of what has become nonsense, especially if its charter was limited to recodifying existing law to accomplish the original intent. In the process, all specialized references to industries and processes could be eliminated. The new law could resolve the conflicts that currently exist in the various forms of protection:

To protect inventions, not goods

1. Patents would be available for all inventions that are nontrivial, nonobvious, and unique, only laws of nature being excluded. Software, algorithms, and other nontrivial processes would obviously be included.

To dovetail the rights

2. Copyright, patent, and trade secret legislation would identify the rights conveyed by each; conflicts between each would be eliminated. Copyright deposits would be either eliminated (most countries do not require deposit) or provision for secure deposit would be provided. It would be made clear that patent application voids trade secrecy rights but that trade secrets and copyrights can coexist.

To prevent *all* harmful copying

3. A "copy" would be defined broadly to insure copyright protection of transliterations, transformations, derivatives, and variants of the original work. All property, not just writings and other works added by Congress, would be subject to copyright.

To define "fair use"

4. "Fair use" of copyright and trade secret material would be spelled out. Use of copyrighted or trade secret material to in any way reduce the commercial potential of the original would not be "fair."

And to give consistent notice

5. The proper form of notice to protect patent, copyright, and trade secrecy rights would be specified; notice conflicts would be eliminated.

A big step . . .

The foregoing is a big step—one that probably will not be taken until the crises in protecting new forms of industrial and intellectual property grow even larger. In the interim, the press for unique changes of the law to accommodate one special interest group or another continue to accumulate. One day it is the distributors of home videotapes seeking unique legislation to increase the punishment of "video pirates." The next day it is the chip manufacturers seeking unique protections for their "masks." Then it is the software industry requesting a means of registering trade secret materials for copyright.

Which won't happen overnight

This pattern will continue until all of the participants recognize that pressing for their special needs only lessens the chance of real success. Until a leader steps forward, however, the special interest legislation will continue. Some recent proposals have been good, some bad, and none have attempted to address the long-term need for legislative overhaul. It is worth examining these individual proposals briefly as they are far more likely to demand your attention in the next several years than broader attacks on the general problem.

Special Interest Legislation

1. The so called "ADAPSO Proposal" (other trade associations participated and supported the proposal) was introduced in the House of Representatives in 1981 by Congressman Robert Kastenmeier (H.R. 6983). The proposal is still extant although the bill has not been reintroduced. This modest legislation would remove several of the ambiguities created by the 1976 and 1980 revisions to the Copyright Act. The act would:

Secure deposit

   a. Mandate a system of secure deposit for works that the copyright holder claimed were confidential. The Copyright Office currently has rule-making authority to do this without legislation, but the bill's sponsors feel a Congressional mandate would be preferable.

Broadly define "software"

   b. Broaden the definition of a program to incorporate all of the forms that software can take (i.e., beyond the set of instructions originally written by the author). The Copyright Office and others consider the transliteration of a program from one form to another (e.g., from source code to object code) to be the making of a copy, hence a protected right, but there continues to be judicial debate and confusion on this point. As more computer-aided programming systems are developed (e.g., programs that translate block diagrams and other design criteria into programs), this issue will grow. The proposal would clarify the issue by defining software broadly enough to insure that any transliteration of the author's work is a copy for copyright purposes.

Make "(c)" legitimate

   c. Make the character string (c) an acceptable form of notice. While this would only be useful in the United States until international treaties were modified, it would be a first step toward a machine-processable copyright notice. There are already three other forms of notice acceptable within the United States, but the only form of notice covered by international treaty, the "c" in a circle, is a special character from a data processing standpoint.

**Reaffirm copy-
right + trade secrecy**

d. Restate Congress's intent that copyright should never pre-empt the nonequivalent rights provided by state trade secrecy laws. The major argument against this proposal is that it is unnecessary, Congress's intentions being clearly spelled out in the legislative history of the Copyright Act revisions. The argument for the revision is that this remains an area of judicial uncertainty and the very uncertainty may be restraining software investment. The ADAPSO proposal is simply a technical amendment to the Copyright Act and as such it has considerable merit and little opposition.

No strong consensus

2. Chip protection legislation has been introduced in various forms over the past six years in both houses of Congress. The legislation has been controversial, even within the semiconductor industry. Basically, these various bills would implement a new form of protection for masks used in the production of chips. Although, as was pointed out in Chapter 5, firmware has been held to be subject to copyright, confusion reigns with regard to the pattern of the electronic components on the chip, a costly part of the chip's development cost.

**...For a new form of
protection
for chips...**

Legislation introduced by Representative Don Edwards in 1978 (H.R. 14293), 1979 (H.R. 1007), and 1982 (H.R. 7207, also introduced in the Senate by Senators Mathias and Hart as S. 1201) would modify the Copyright Act to provide special ten-year copyright protection to chips. The rights conveyed would cover the right to make, use, and sell or "substantially to reproduce" (i.e., rights far beyond normal copyright protections but not quite those conveyed by a patent).

**...And some
strong opposition**

Although the plight of the chip manufacturers is real, millions of look-alike chips having been fabricated and sold, the support for these bills has been less than overwhelming. The major opposition has come from those who fear that a third class of hybrid protections, neither copyright nor patent, could weaken these basic concepts. A second source of opposition has come from those who feel that existing copyright protections should be sufficient for masks, which are included under the protections afforded "pictorial, graphic, and sculptural works." This group feels the semiconductor industry should press for judicial redress under the existing law, despite anticipated setbacks while the courts resolve the issues, rather than pressing for special legislation.

The chip manufacturers point out that you cannot have a copyright on a "useful article." (This, so the theory goes, would create a monopoly never anticipated in our Constitution or by Congress when it passed the Copyright Act.) But, is it really the useful article (i.e., the chip itself) that the chip manufacturer wants to protect or the use of his or her original work (i.e., the mask layout)? The fact that the resulting article contains a copy of a copyrighted work should be sufficient. If a sculptor has a copyright on all of the castings he or she makes and the artist has a copyright on his or her lithographs, why should the chip manufacturer be treated differently?

But the need is real

In the final analysis, however, lacking a complete copyright revision, some legislative tinkering may be necessary to protect masks. An intelligent interim step might be to simply reaffirm the applicability of copyright to mask patterns as pictorial, graphic, or sculptural works. This would leave the copyright owner with the burden of proving that another chip embodied either a copy or a derivative of the copyrighted mask, but this, of course, is the burden every copyright owner must bear.

All pirates should hang equally high

3. Special "piracy legislation" was introduced in 1982 (H.R. 6420) to increase the statutory penalties for copyright infringement and counterfeiting of software. In 1981, Title 18 of the federal statutes was changed to increase the statutory penalties for criminal copyright infringement, specifically as they apply to motion pictures, sound recordings, and other audio-visual works. Under these revisions the maximum criminal penalty rose to $250,000 and five years in prison. Based on the aforementioned ambiguities in the much-modified Copyright Act, it is unclear whether these increased penalties could apply to software or not. The proposed legislation would have added software to the itemized list of items covered by the increased penalties.

A technical revision . . .

This legislation, like the ADAPSO proposal, was essentially a technical amendment to the law, and as such it excited little interest. With a geometric increase occurring in the number of software copyright cases, however, there is a reasonable expectation that this legislation will resurface.

Illustrating the need for a complete rewrite

Valuable as it might be in its own right, legislation like this illustrates what a hodgepodge the Copyright Act has become. Why should the criminal penalties applicable to one form of industrial piracy be different than any other? Why does the Copyright Act have to be revised every time a new form of "writing" appears on the scene? (There is considerable pressure, for example, to add "databases" to the itemized list of protected works.) While it would be hard to argue against the need for parity in our criminal penalties, it is even easier to argue the need for restoring sanity to our venerable and valuable Copyright Act.

Modify the "first sale" doctrine

4. Although originally raised by the recording and motion picture industry, the debate over the so-called "first sale" doctrine has implications for software. Under this doctrine, copyrighted material may be sold or rented without additional financial liability to the copyright owner. In many cases, as in the renting of home video recordings, this can put the commercial renter in direct competition with the copyright holder.

To give copyright holders control over rentals

A proposal sponsored by the government would bar commercial rental of copyrighted material without the prior permission of the copyright holder. At present these bills are specifically proposed for sound recordings and audio-visual works, but, as repetitively noted, the distinctions between "works of authorship" are fading. In addition, there is building pressure from microcomputer software producers to similarly limit "rentals" of software, which they see as an organized effort to promote theft (rent it, copy it, return it).

Care is called for

As with all the other special-interest legislation, these proposals need more thought. Do we really want the author or artist involved in every downstream transaction involving a copyrighted work? Is this really a copyright issue? If you buy a work of art, for example, should you have to get the artist's permission before you sell it, put it on exhibition, or otherwise dispose of it?

Other Issues

There are two other issues worth including in this discussion of public policy and the future of software protection, both related to software exports. The international market for software is exploding. To keep this market alive and healthy, an issue of critical concern to U.S. firms who have, to date, dominated the world market for software, urgent revisions are required in international copyright treaties. In addition, the U.S. government must take a rational position on the issue of limiting technology exports, most notably software, that could have military or political value to our enemies.

The world needs updated copyright treaties

The United States has always been a leader in revising its copyright law to incorporate new technologies (hence the current need for a complete rewrite to clean up all the loose ends). The United States was the first to make computer programs a specifically protected work, something that has been left to judicial interpretation in most other countries. While it is reasonable to expect that eventually all countries will agree to a single rational standard for cross-border copyright protection of software, it would be far better if an international agreement could be reached *now*.

The U.S. should take the lead

The United States is in a position to play a major role in such an undertaking: Today we have technological and economic leadership on our side. Misguided rulings that software is not subject to copyright, or national decisions to erect import barriers by deliberately putting software in a protected category are fortunately rare, recent, and reversible. However, time is a factor. The sooner an international agreement is reached on protection of software by copyright, the better for *everyone*.

. . . On the issue of export controls

The issue of national security is also a real one; no one would doubt that our missile guidance software could have incalculable value to an enemy. But does our commercially available software have military or political benefit? And, if so, does restricting its distribution have benefits that outweigh the costs? I think not.

Most commmercial software is one generation behind

Most software products have a life of less than five years. Even within that five-year period the products are continually revised to incorporate new functions, to respond to hardware changes, and to correct errors. While one product is being marketed another is under development; each successful product carries the seeds of its own replacement. In general, the products a software company is developing in its laboratories are from two to five years ahead of the products it is marketing.

Competitive offerings are available abroad

In addition, a successful software product breeds international competition. Admittedly, the U.S. software industry has dominated the world market, but this does not mean that you cannot buy a functional equivalent for nearly every U.S. software product from a non-U.S. source.

Controls reduce profits without creating effective barriers

Given these conditions, what is the net effect of restricting commercial software sales abroad by requiring (1) a license for each sale in a restricted territory, and (2) contractual guarantees from all customers that they will not resell the product in a restricted territory? The answer is reduced U.S. exports, no real penalties on our enemies (who either steal the software or buy it legitimately elsewhere), and an eventual weakening of our worldwide competitive (and hence military) position. In addition, the software we hope to have denied our enemies is so far out of date as to be of no possible strategic benefit.

A true-life example

In 1980 my company was asked to bid on a sale of telecommunications software to the agency that served the Hungarian government's data processing needs. The software in question had been on the market since 1970 (an extraordinary life for a software product).

The software was old and tired, and had many competitors, foreign as well as domestic. After four months of delay in attempting to get an export license, the prospect awarded a multimillion-dollar contract to a British competitor.

I submit that we must rationalize our export licensing procedures. If export licenses are to be required for commercial software products at all, of dubious benefit at best, the licensing procedures should be on a product-by-product, not a sale-by-sale basis. The Commerce Department, which is charged with promoting exports abroad, should be given the charter of coordinating and expediting the award of licenses. This will happen only if the business community demands it.

If needed, licenses should be by product, not by sale

Conclusion

There would have been no point for this book if the issues of software protection were all settled. Furthermore, I do not anticipate a rapid resolution of many of these: The business community itself is not yet fully educated on the issues and has not taken clear and consistent positions on its needs. Similarly, our legislators and courts can only react to well-articulated arguments, and only a handful of lawyers are equipped to deal with these relatively new and arcane issues. In brief, anticipate a continued state of turmoil.

You can survive the turmoil, however. Take charge of the process in your own organization. Hire one of the few experts in the field or make sure that your attorney becomes one. Get active in one or more trade associations or industry groups so at least you will know of and can intelligently react to legislative proposals that may affect your livelihood. Follow the precepts I have tried to lay out in this book until better ones come along.

Agent	An individual or company authorized to perform narrowly specified acts for someone, e.g., to make sales and provide services, as contrasted to a "distributor."
Algorithm	A step-by-step procedure, formula, set of rules, or process to produce a desired result, calculation, or output. The U.S. Supreme Court, in *Benson*[23] and in *Flook*[27] used a narrower definition, i.e., a "procedure for solving a given type of mathematical formula."
Application software	Software which performs useful work for the computer user (in contrast to system software), e.g., the calculation of a payroll.
Assemble	Conversion of a program written in high-level symbols into the native language of the computer. See also *Compile*.
Certiorari	Granting of a review of a lower court's decision by the U.S. Supreme Court.
Chip	A piece of a (generally) silicon crystal that has been etched according to the pattern on a mask, forming multiple electronic components into a single electronic device, e.g., a microcomputer or a memory bank.
COBOL	A high-level programming language for business applications (COmmon Business Oriented Language). COBOL source programs must be compiled into object programs.
Code	Program instructions. Usually qualified as either source code or object code.

Compile	Transliteration of a source program into an object program, usually by means of another program called a "compiler."
Consequential damages	The downstream losses suffered as the result of a defective product's use, e.g., if a product burns down a factory, the cost of replacing the factory would be *direct* but the profits lost while it was closed would *consequential*.
Consideration	That which is given up by a party to a contract in return for that which is given up by the other parties. In general, for a valid contract to exist between two parties, there must be consideration on both sides.
Courseware	An educational program packaged for machine delivery, usually under program control.
Disk	A circular plate, coated with a metallic oxide, on which information can be recorded. While the disk is rotated, a disk drive either writes information to the disk by selectively magnetizing different areas, or reads previously recorded information by sensing changes in magnetization.
Disk drive	A peripheral device used to store and subsequently retrieve information recorded magnetically on rotating disks.
Distributor	A company or individual who buys for their own account and then resells through a wholesale or retail distribution network.
Dump	The character-by-character printout of the contents of a computer's memory.
Encryption	The translation of one character string into another by means of a cypher, translation table, or algorithm, in order to render the information contained in the character string meaningless to anyone not possessing the decoding mechanism.
Firmware	Software delivered as part of or stored in a machine component, usually a memory device, e.g., ROM.
Floppy disk	A supple disk, usually protected by a plastic sleeve, that can be removed from the disk drive.
FORTRAN	A high-level programming language primarily used for engineering and scientific applications. FORTRAN source programs must be compiled into object programs.
Hard disk	One or more disks that are hermetically sealed with the disk drive's read/write unit in order to increase storage capacity, speed of access, and reliability.
Hardware	The tangible components of a computer system.
Implied warranty	A warranty granted to a purchaser by the force of law rather than by the vendor. Implied warranties usually cover a product's "merchantability and fitness for a given purpose," i.e., the (generally retail) buyer's right to expect that the product will perform the function for which it was sold.

Injunction	A court order restraining a particular act, usually until the issues being disputed can be brought to trial.
Innocent infringement	The copying of a work that, as a result of missing notice, is not a violation of law.
Instruction	The smallest logical component of a computer program, sometimes called a "statement" or a "line of code."
Intangible	Incorporeal; unable to be perceived by the senses when separated from a tangible medium.
Intellectual property	Intangible property produced through a creative process, e.g., by drawing, composing, writing, or arranging.
License agreement	A contract granting otherwise restricted rights (e.g., to use a trade secret) to a third party.
Mask	The pattern used to etch an electronic circuit into a silicon wafer; the critical transfer of intellectual property in the manufacture of electronic chips.
Memory	An integral part of a computer system designed to temporarily store programs and data while the computer operates, as opposed to more permanent external storage, such as tape or disk, which can store information separate from the computer's operation.
Microcomputer	A miniaturized computer system based on one or more "computers on a chip," i.e., a programmable processor implemented in a single chip of silicon. Microcomputers generally are sold as a complete system, including additional chip-level electronic storage (i.e., "memory") and peripheral devices (e.g., a display monitor, a keyboard, disk storage, and a printer).
Object code	See *Object program*.
Object program	A program that has been written in or compiled into the native programming language of particular hardware. Object programs can also be source programs.
On-line	Availability or use of a computer or peripheral device on an interactive basis, i.e., by one or more individuals, usually through keyboard entry and display output.
Operating system	A program that controls the scheduling, initialization, and execution of other programs, while providing support services that simplify or eliminate the need for those programs to repeat commonly used tasks, e.g., instructing the computer how to print a line of information from an area in memory.
Peripheral device	An input/output device that is connected to a computer by a cable, e.g., a disk drive, a printer.
Pirate	An overly romantic term that is currently in vogue to describe someone who illegally copies the intellectual property of someone else.
Publication	A defined term under the Copyright Act, meaning the distribution of copies by sale, rental, lease, or lending.

Public domain	Intellectual property enters the public domain, i.e., that point at which the public at large has a right to copy and use it, when it has lost its copyright or other legal protections.
Reverse engineering	The creation of a competitive offering by the minute examination of an existing product, e.g., by disassembling something into its component parts to study its design.
ROM	Read-Only Memory. A semi-permanent or permanent computer storage device used to store, most frequently, system software.
Software	A computer program plus its descriptive and supporting materials. See Chapter 2.
Source code	See *Source program*.
Source program	A program as originally written by the programmer. A source program may also be an object program.
Statement	A single program instruction.
Sui generis	Unique; one of a kind.
System software	Software used by or which controls other software.
Tangible	That which can can be seen, weighed, measured, felt, or touched.
Track	One of many concentric circles defined on the face of a disk as information is recorded. Most disk devices move the recording device to discrete positions away from the center of the disk's rotation in order to better use the recording surface, hence creating tracks of information.
Trade secret	Any business information that, because it is maintained in confidence, provides a competitive advantage. See Chapter 6.
Uniform Commercial Code (UCC)	A standardized consumer protection law that has been adopted by most of the states to govern retail transactions.
Videodisk	A sealed disk on which digitized sound, pictures, programs, animation, data, etc., have been recorded, most commonly by etching the disk's silvered surface with a laser. The etched bits may then be read back by reflecting a second laser beam to an intensity detector.
WIPO	The World Intellectual Property Organization. A United Nations agency headquartered in Geneva that administers international treaties on intellectual property.
Work for hire	A work prepared by an employee within the scope of his or her employment, or a work specially ordered or commissioned, in a written agreement, as a work made for hire.

REFERENCES

1. *Model Provisions of the Protection of Computer Software,* World Intellectual Property Organization (WIPO), Geneva, 1978.

   (ADAPSO and others have recommended replacing the current Copyright Act's definition of "program" with WIPO's more inclusive definition of "software." WIPO's position paper notes, "A program description can be considered computer software if it covers all of the steps to be taken in the execution of a computer program.... This means that the program description sets out all of the instructions to be followed by the computer so that the only thing that remains to be done is to convert them into a form that is acceptable to the computer." Clearly, detailed block diagrams and/or decision tables would be considered "software" under these tests.)

2. *73 Corpus Juris Secundum* 156 (1942).

3. *Statement of Financial Accounting Standards No. 2, Accounting for Research and Development Costs,* Financial Accounting Standards Board, October 1978; and *FASB Interpretation No. 6, Applicability of FASB Statement No. 2 to Computer Software,* Financial Accounting Standards Board, February 1975.

   (The basic definitions of "research" and "development" as set forth in Statement No. 2 are:

" *'Research'* is planned search or critical investigation aimed at discovery or new knowledge with the hope that such knowledge will be useful in developing a new product or service . . . . *'Development'* is the translation of research findings into a plan or design for a new product or process . . . ."

As this relates to computer software, *Interpretation No. 6* added:

" . . . Costs incurred for *conceptual formulation or the translation of knowledge into a design* would be research and development costs (see paragraph 8 of Statement No. 2). Other costs, including those for programming and testing software, are research and development costs when incurred in the search for or the evolution of product or process alternatives or in the design of a preproduction model. On the other hand, costs for programming and testing are *not* research and development costs when incurred, for example, in routine or other on-going efforts to improve an existing product . . . ."

With regard to the purchase or lease of software, *Interpretation No. 6* states:

"Costs incurred to purchase or lease computer software developed by others are not research and development costs."

As they relate to a software company's normal activities, these guidelines state:

1. Investigations, preliminary designs, feasibility analyses, and other product research costs *must* be expensed in the period in which they are incurred.

2. The acquisition of a product from a third party *plus* the costs of repackaging, redocumenting, or enhancing the acquired product are not research and development expenses and thus *may* be capitalized and amortized over the product's useful life.

3. Routine enhancement of an existing product (a large percentage of most software companies' technical expenditures) are not research and development expense and *may* be capitalized.)

The FASB recently (file reference 1007-022, published 8/31/84) proposed making mandatory the previously optional portions of these guidelines, effective 12/15/84. From that date, the cost of producing product masters, including coding and testing, will be capitalized when recoverability of these costs has been established.

4. Forms and instructions are available from the Information and Publications Section, LM-455, Copyright Office, Library of Congress, Washington, D.C. 20559. A "hot line" service is available to order forms twenty-four hours a day at (202) 287-9100, and information is available from the Copyright Public Information Office weekdays from 8:30 A.M. through 5.00 P.M at (202) 287-8700.

5. Act of Feb. 21, 1793, Ch. 11, Par. 1, 1 Stat. 318.

6. S. Rep. No. 1979, 82d Cong., 2d Sess., 5 (1952).

7. *Corning* v. *Burder,* 15 How. 252, 267–268 (1853).

>("The arts of tanning, dyeing, making waterproof cloth, vulcaniz-ing india rubber, smelting ores, and numerous others, are usually carried out by a process as distinguished from machines. One may discover a new and useful improvement in the process . . . irre-spective of any particular form of machinery or mechanical de-vice . . . . It is for the discovery or invention of some practical meth-od or means of producing a beneficial result or effect, that a patent is granted and not for the result of effect itself. It is when the term process is used to represent the means or method of producing a re-sult that it is patentable and it will include all methods or means which are not affected by mechanism or mechanical connota-tions.")

8. *Cochrane* v. *Deemer,* 94 U.S. 780, 787–788 (1876).

>("That a process may be patentable, irrespective of the particular form of the instrumentalities used, cannot be disputed . . . a process is a mode of treatment of certain materials to produce a given re-sult. It is an act, or a series of acts, performed on the subject matter to be transformed and reduced to a different state or thing.")

9. *Gottschalk* v. *Benson,* 409 U.S. 63, 67 (1973); 175 USPQ 673 (1972); and *Mackay Radio and Telephone Co.* v. *Radio Corp. of America,* 306 U.S. 86, 94, 40; USPQ 199, 202 (1939).

10. 35 U.S.C 101.

11. The European Patent Convention, concluded in Munich on October 5, 1973, Art. 52(2)(c) states that " . . . programs for computers . . . " are not subject to patents. While not binding on member countries, both France and the United Kingdom have adopted restrictive legislation implementing the Convention's intent. French Patent Law No. 78-479 (1978) disallows the patenting of pure software, as does the United Kingdom Patents Act of 1977 which excludes (Par. 1 at 2(c)): "a scheme, rule or method for performing a mental act, playing a game or doing business, or a program for a computer."

12. *Diamond* v. *Diehr,* 450 U.S. 175, 209 USPQ 1(1981), 519 PTCJ AA-1, D-1.

13. *In re Abrams,* 188 F.2d 165 (CCPA, 1951).

14. *In re Prater,* 415 F. 2d. 1378 (CCPA, 1968), modified on rehearing, 415 F. 2d. 1393 (CCPA, 1969).

15. *In re Bernhart and Fetter,* 417 F. 2d. 1395 (CCPA, 1969).

16. *Mackay Radio and Telephone Co.* v. *Radio Corp. of America,* 306 U.S. 86, 94; 40 USPQ 199, 202 (1939).

    (This case held that "while a scientific truth or the mathematical expression of it is not a patentable invention, a novel and useful structure created with the aid of a scientific truth may be.")

17. *Corning* v. *Burder.*

18. *Report of the President's Commission on the Patent System, "To Promote the Process of. . . Useful Arts" in an Age of Exploding Technology* 13 (1966).

19. *In re Tarczy-Hornoch,* 397 F. 2d 856 (CCPA, 1968).

20. *Diamond* v. *Diehr.*

21. *In re Abrams.*

22. *In re Musgrave,* 431 F. 2d 882 (CCPA, 1970).

23. *In re Benson,* 441 F. 2d 682 (CCPA, 1971).

24. *Gottschalk* v. *Benson,* 409 U.S. 63,67 (1973); 175 USPQ 673 (1972).

25. *In re Johnston,* 502 F. 2d 765 (CCPA, 1974). *In re Noll,* 545 F. 2d 141 (CCPA, 1976). *In re Chatfield,* 545 F. 2d 152 (CCPA, 1976).

26. *In re Freeman,* 573 F. 2d 1237 (CCPA, 1978).

27. *In re Flook,* 559 F. 2d 21 (CCPA, 1977), reversed in *Parker* v. *Flook,* 437 U.S. 584 (1978).

28. Ibid.

    ("The notion that post-solution activity, no matter how conventional or obvious in itself, can transform an unpatentable principle into a patentable process exalts form over substance. A competent draftsman could attach some form of post-solution activity to almost any mathematical formula: the Pythagoren theorem would not have been patentable, or partially patentable, because a patent application contained a final step indicating that the formula, when solved could be usefully applied to existing suryveying techniques.")

29. *In re Johnson,* 589 F. 2d 1070 (CCPA, 1978).

    (This case is especially interesting (see 200 USPQ at 210, 211) in that it affirmed that computer implemented "processes are encompassed within 35 USC 101 under the same principles as other machine implemented processes, subject to judicially determined exceptions, inter alia, mathematical formulas (sic), methods of calculation, and mere ideas.")

    See also *In re Phillips,* 608 F. 2d 879 (CCPA, 1979); and *In re Sherwood,* 613 F. 2d 809 (CCPA, 1980).

30. *Diamond* v. *Bradley,* 450 U.S. 381 (1981).

31. 17 U.S.C. 106.

32. *1976 Copyright Act,* Title 17 of U.S. Code, Sections 401–412, P.L. 94-553, 90 Stat. 2541.

33. *H.R. Rep. No. 94-1476,* 94th Cong., 2nd Sess. 61 (1976) reprinted in *U.S. Code Cong. and Admin. News* 5659 (1976); and *S. Rep. No. 94-473,* 94th Cong., 1st Sess. 58 (1975).

34. *Computer and Software Copyright Act,* P.L. 96-517, 94 Stat. 3015 amending U.S.C. 101, 117.

35. *Final Report of the National Commission of New Technological Uses of Copyrighted Works,* July 31, 1978.

36. See *New York Times Co.* v. *Roxbury Data Interface, Inc.,* 434 F. Supp. 217 (D. N.J., 1977); and *Jewelers' Circular Publishing Co.* v. *Keystone Publishing Co.,* F. 83 (3rd Cir., 1922).

37. *H.R. Rep. No. 94-1476;* and *S. Rep. No. 94-473.*

38 17 U.S.C 401(c).

39. *Methods of Affixation and Positions of the Copyright Notice,* 37 C.F.R. 201, Rm 77-14A.

40. *Technican Medical Information Systems Corp.* v. *Green Bay Packaging, Inc.,* 78-C-363 (E.D. Wisc., 1980), Corp. L. Rep. (CCH) 25.255.

41. See *Methods of Affixation and Positions,* at 201.20(g).

42. 37 C.F.R. at 202.19(c)(5), 1978.

43. 17 U.S.C. 412.

44. 17 U.S.C. 407(c) and 408(c).

45. Relief can be requested from the Chief, Acquisitions and Processing Division, U.S. Copyright Office, Library of Congress, Washington D.C.

46. Letter to the author from Dorothy Schrader, General Counsel, Copyright Office, dated February 2, 1984.

47. Ibid.

48. The Copyright Office's authority to keep information confidential, specifically "secure tests," was upheld in *National Conference of Bar Examiners and Educational Service* v. *Multistate Legal Services, Inc.* 629 F. 2d. 478 (7th Cir., 1982). On May 23, 1983, the Copyright Office circulated an inquiry on the possibility of similar treatment for software containing confidential information. No decision has yet been published.

49. *Midway Manufacturing Co.* v. *Drikschneider,* reported in 541 Pat., T.M. & Copyright J. (BNA), August 13, 1981 at A-3.

50. *Tandy Corp.* v. *Personal Micro Computers, Inc.,* 524 F. Supp. 171 (N.D. Cal., 1981).

51. *Williams Electronics, Inc.* v. *Artic International, Inc.,* 685 F. 2d 870 (3rd Cir. 1982).

52. *GCA Corp.* v. *Chance,* No. C82-1063 MHP (N.D. Cal. 1982); and *Hubco Data Products Corp.* v. *Management Assistance, Inc.,* No. 81-1295 (D. Idaho, Feb 3, 1983); and *Apple Computer, Inc.* v. *Formula International, Inc.,* No. CV 82-5015-IH (C.D. Cal. 1983).

53. *Stern Electronics, Inc.* v. *Kaufman,* 213 U.S.P.Q. 75 (E.D. N.Y. 1981), aff'd 669 F. 2d 852 (2d Cir. 1982).

54. *Actes de la 3em Conférence Internationale pour la Protection des Oeuvres littéraires et Artistiques, réunie a Berne de 6 au 9 Septembre 1886* (known as the "Berne Convention"), revised in Berlin (1908), Rome (1928), Brussels (1948), Stockholm (1967), and Paris (1971); and *The Universal Copyright Convention,* Sept. 6, 1952, U.N.T.S. 2937, T.I.A.S. No. 7868 (drafted under UNESCO auspices at Geneva, revised (in conjunction with the Berne Convention) in Paris, 1971).

55. *In re Certain Coin-Operated Audio Visual Games and Components Thereof,* International Trade Commission (Docket No. 337-TA-87, June 26, 1981 at A-5).

56. *The Restatement of Torts,* 757 (b) 1939.

57. *Comshare, Inc.* v. *Computer Complex, Inc.,* 338 F. Supp. 1229 (E.D. Mich., 1971).

58. "Matters of public knowledge or of general knowledge in...industry cannot be appropriated by one as his secret" (*Sperry Rand Corp.* v. *Pentronix,* 311 F. Supp, 910,913 (E.D. Pa., 1970)).
    See also *Kewanee Oil Co.* v. *Bicron Corp.,* 416 U.S. 475 (1974).

59. *Abbot Laboratories* v. *Norse Chemical Corp.,* 33 Wis. 2d 445, 447 (1967).

60. "It is not necessary that a trade secret be absolutely secret; qualified secrecy is sufficient" (*E. W. Bliss Company* v. *Struthers-Dunn Inc.,* 291 F. Supp. 390, 400 (S.D. Iowa, 1968)).

61. *Wexler* v. *Greenberg,* 399 Pa. 569, 160 A. 2d. 430 (1960).

62. *BPI Systems, Inc.* v. *Leith Commodore Computer Co.,* 532 F. Supp 208 (W.D. Tex 1981).

63. See *Sears Roebuck and Co.* v. *Stiffel and Co.,* 376 U.S. 225 (1964); and *Compco Corp.* v. *Day-Brite Lighting,* 376 U.S. 234 (1964).

64. *Kewanee Oil Co.* v. *Bicron Corp.,* 416 U.S. 470 (1974).

65. *Final Report of the National Commission of New Technological Uses of Copyrighted Works,* July 31, 1978.

66. *H. Rep. #94-1476,* 94th. Cong., 2nd Sess. 132 (1976), reprinted in *U.S. Code Cong. Admin. News* 5746-5747.

67. *Warrington Associates, Inc.* v. *Real-Time Engineering Systems, Inc.,* (N.D. Ill. 1981), 552 PTCJ A-6.

68. *Technican Medical Information Systems Corp.* v. *Green Bay Packaging, Inc.,* 78-C-363 (E.D. Wisc., 1980), Corp. L. Rep. (CCH) 25.255; see also *Management Science America, Inc.* v. *Cyborg Systems, Inc.,* 76-C-2149 (N.D. Ill. 6/8/78).

69. See reference 54 at 759.

70. See *Plant Industries, Inc. Coleman,* 287 F. Supp. 636 (D.C. Cal. 1968).

71. See *Winston Research Corp.* v. *Minnesota Mining and Manufacturing,* 350 F. 2d 134, 142 (9th Cir. 1965); and *Analogic* v. *Datatranslation, Inc.,* 358 N.E. 804,807 (Mass. 1976).

72. See *Wexler* v. *Greenberg,* 399 Pa. 569, 160A. 2d 430 (1960).

73. See the California ruling *Diodes* v. *Franzen,* 260 Cal. App. 2d 244, 260 (1968).

> ("One who seeks protection . . . of a trade secret must plead facts showing (1) the existence of . . . a trade secret; (2) . . . a contractual or other legally imposed obligation . . . not to use or disclose the secret . . . and (3) . . . the complainant's interest in maintaining the secret outweighs the interest of the employee in using his knowledge to support himself in other employment.")

74. See *Triangle Underwriters, Inc.* v. *Honeywell Information Systems, Inc.,* 604 F. 2d 737 (2d Cir., 1979); and *Carl Beasley Ford, Inc.* v. *Burroughs Corp.,* 361 F. Supp. 325 (Pa., 1975); and *Chatlos Systems, Inc. (CSI)* v. *NCR Corp.,* 479 F. Supp. 738 (N.J., 1979).

75. Available from the Association of Data Processing Service Organizations (ADAPSO), 1300 N. 17th Street, Arlington, Va. 22209-3899.

76. See *Model Provisions of the Protection of Computer Software,* World Intellectual Property Organization (WIPO), Geneva, 1978.

INDEX